GUN SAINT

By John Michael Snyder

Telum Associates, L.L.C.
Arlington, Virginia

GUN SAINT, Copyright 2003 by John Michael Snyder

Published by Telum Associates, Arlington, Virginia

ISBN 0-9728756-0-3

to

Ling

Table of Contents

Chapter 1: The Shot	1
Chapter 2: The Evidence	4
Chapter 3: "At Last, A Pistol Saint"	7
Chapter 4: What is a Saint?	12
Chapter 5: What is a Patron Saint?	16
Chapter 6: Why a Patron Saint for Handgunners?	19
Chapter 7: Why Designate St. Gabriel Possenti the Patron of Handgunners?	34
Chapter 8: Some Negative Reaction	38
Chapter 9: Founding the St. Gabriel Possenti Society, Inc.	45
Chapter 10: Shooting Facility Dedicated to St. Gabriel Possenti	51
Chapter 11: Controversy Surrounding the Dedication	54

Chapter 12:	Fatuous Bishops	61
Chapter 13:	A Good Bishop	66
Chapter 14:	A Good Christian Minister	69
Chapter 15:	Armed Catholic Nuns	73
Chapter 16:	Genocide	76
Chapter 17:	Visiting Isola del Gran Sasso	80
Chapter 18:	A Call From a Possenti	85
Chapter 19:	Rome Conference	91
Chapter 20:	Send Them a Message	98
Chapter 21:	Presentation to the Chairman of the Joint Chiefs of Staff	101
Chapter 22:	Rev. Cirilo Nacorda	104
Chapter 23:	An Age of Peril	110
Appendix A:	Prayer from an Anonymous Source	114
Appendix B:	Prayer Composed by the Author	115

Appendix C: Firearms: The Handgun Saint:
Gabriel Possenti 116

Appendix D: Pistol Packin' Piety: A Patron
Saint for Handgunners? 120

Appendix E: American Handgunners to Seek
Vatican Recognition 124

Chapter 1

The Shot

The bullet from the .36 caliber cap and ball revolver slammed into the reptile's head and the lizard rolled over, dead as a doornail!

The hand holding the Italian knock-off of the 1851 Colt Navy Model revolver was the blessed hand of a Roman Catholic Saint. St. Gabriel Francis Possenti.

Moments before, the youthful Passionist seminarian has rescued a young village woman from the hands of two would-be rapists.

Moments later, armed with that revolver and another one similar to it, he pointed both of them at a gang of advancing terrorists. The next bullet, he warned them, would be "through your heart" if they did not cease and desist.

They ceased and they desisted.

The incident occurred in 1860 in Isola del Gran Sasso, Italy.

Following a battle that year in Pesaro, in which soldiers of the Piedmontese Army defeated soldiers of the Papal Army loyal to Blessed Pope Pius IX, various contingents of the Piedmontese Army of Giuseppe Garibaldi separated themselves from the main body of troops and became, in effect, renegades.

A number of these groups of renegades then proceeded to terrorize the countryside, stealing the people's property, raping the women and generally pillaging the villages.

One of these groups of terrorists, of about 20 former solders and non-commissioned officers, came upon Isola del Gran Sasso, and proceeded to wreak their havoc on the poor villagers.

Adjacent to Isola there was, and is, a Passionist monastery.

At the time, Possenti was pursuing studies there as a seminarian, studying for the Roman Catholic priesthood.

Prior to entering religious life, Possenti had been quite an outdoorsman, quite a sportsman. He was known to be proficient in the use of various kinds of firearms, rifles and shotguns as well as handguns.

When the noise from the ruckus caused by the terrorists reached the monastery, Possenti asked the monastery rector, if he could go into the town to see if he somehow could help the people. The rector, himself so frightened that he had locked up the various monastery chapel valuables, reluctantly gave his consent.

As Possenti raced into town, he saw a sergeant literally about to rape a young woman. To the sergeant's surprise, Possenti yanked the soldier's handgun out of his holster and ordered him to unhand the woman. Possenti did the same to another sergeant, also a would-be rapist. The two of them, dumbfounded, let the woman go.

When the other soldiers in the band of about 20 heard the commotion, they rushed toward Possenti, thinking they easily could make short shrift of this slightly built, cassocked theology student. One of them apparently made some sneering remark about him attired in his cassock.

At that moment, a lizard ran across the road. The marksman Possenti took aim, fired, and killed it with one shot. It was then that he turned his weapons toward the advancing gang, surprised and shocked by this amazing demonstration of handgun marksmanship.

Possenti ordered the terrorists to put down their arms, which they did.

He ordered them to put out the fires that they had started, which they did.

He ordered them to return the property that they had taken from the villagers, which they did.

He then ordered the whole lot of them out of town at gunpoint. They left, never to return.

The Isolans then accompanied Possenti back to his monastery in triumphant procession, naming him the "Savior of Isola."

Chapter 2

The Evidence

Striking as it may seem, the incident described in the previous chapter is historically accurate. Possenti's fellow Passionist, Rev. Godfrey Poage, C. P., recounted most of it in his biography of the Saint, Son of the Passion, The Story of Gabriel Francis Possenti, the New Patron of Catholic Youth, published in 1962 in Milwaukee, Wisconsin by the Bruce Publishing Company. The Daughters of St. Paul published another edition of the same book in 1977 in Boston, Massachusetts.

Father Poage was a peritus, or an expert, advising the Bishops of the Catholic Church who comprised the Second Vatican Council in Rome in the early 1960s. During an earlier, 1947-1948 period in Italy, Father Poage did much of the research for his biography of St. Gabriel Possenti. The book carries two nihil obstats, an imprimi potest, and an imprimatur, certifying that the volume is free of Catholic doctrinal error.

In the introduction, Father Poage explained that in the book, "nothing was said that had not been quoted by eyewitnesses, at least in the third person."

Two items in the previous chapter of the current volume not cited in the Poage book are the fact that the young woman saved from molestation by Possenti actually was at the point of rape by the renegade sergeant, and the fact that Possenti stated to the terrorists as he faced them with the revolvers that the next bullet would be "through your heart." During a September 29, 1992 meeting in Los Angeles, California between Father Poage and me, Father Poage explained that, since his volume originally was intended for youthful audiences, his editors thought it best at the time, in 1962, to provide the young readers with a softened account of the "lizard incident."

In his biography, Father Poage did not go into detail with regard to the kind of pistols the two sergeants were carrying. These were the pistols that Possenti liberated from the renegade sergeants' hands and used in his heroic rescue of Isola.

Mr. Paolo Tagini, Editor of Armi, a universally respected current Italian firearms magazine, researched this matter for me. He reported that, in and around 1860 in Italy, neither military nor civil authorities issued sidearms to military personnel. Such personnel provided themselves with such arms if they wished and could somehow obtain them. At the time, the most popular such sidearm was the 1851 Colt Navy Model six-shot revolver in .36 caliber or imitations thereof. This confirmed an earlier opinion expressed verbally to me by Mr. Val Forgett, Founder of Navy Arms, and a nationally recognized authority on antique firearms and reproductions of antique firearms.

Rev. Clifford Stevens included his account of the 1860 lizard incident in The One Year Book of Saints, published in 1989 by the Our Sunday Visitor Publishing Division of Our Sunday Visitor, Inc. in Huntington, Indiana. Father Stevens noted St. Gabriel Possenti in connection with his Feast Day, February 27.

Earlier, in 1983, Ms. Ann Ball included her account of the same incident in her book, Modern Saints, Their Lives and Faces, published by Tan Books and Publishers, Inc. of Rockford, Illinois.

By 1987, New Covenant magazine featured an adaptation of the Ball account in its February issue, in its Lives of the Saints section, in conjunction with the February 27 Feast Day of St. Gabriel Possenti.

Chapter 3

"At Last, A Pistol Saint"

The New Covenant magazine article actually was the beginning of my formal awareness of St. Gabriel Possenti and the "lizard incident."

Years before, during my adolescence, my mother's godson, Rev. Bernard Quilty, C.SS.R., had told me about the incident in passing, but it had long since passed from my mind.

After reading the New Covenant article, I sent a copy of it along to Mr. Joseph P. Tartaro, Executive Editor of The New Gun Week.

Mr. Tartaro was so impressed with the account that he made it the subject of his April 17, 1987 weekly Hindsight column, which he headlined as "At Last, A Pistol Saint."

"Now that I know something about St. Gabriel Possenti," wrote Mr. Tartaro, "I'm sorry it has taken me so long to learn about him. And, while he was named the patron saint of Catholic youth by Pope Benedict XV, the story in the New Covenant suggests he might also be the patron saint of handgunners, if not those who would use guns for defense of themselves or others."

Mr. Tartaro indicated that, "what I find particularly interesting is that this young man, whom the church later proclaimed a saint, used a handgun to successfully defend people in trouble. While he fired a shot, he didn't actually have to kill anyone. The presence of a pistol, in the hand of someone who obviously knew how to use it, was enough to deter crime and violence. From the story, however, it is clear that St. Gabriel would have used the handgun to shoot the predatory criminals if in 'the gravest extreme.' But the presence of the handgun was enough to do the trick.

"The New Covenant does not report whether there were anti-gun researchers around at the time of the incident in Italy. If so, they would have written off the saint's actions because there was no body count to compare with the number of incidents in which 'family and friends' were killed with handguns...He was a very young man when he died, but St. Gabriel deserves to be remembered by those who support the cause of private ownership of small arms."

Taking a cue from the Hindsight column, and discovering through research that the Catholic Church indeed had not designated officially a Patron Saint of Handgunners, I wrote a letter on May 1, 1987, the Feast of St. Joseph the Worker, to the Cardinal Prefect of the Sacred Congregation for the Causes of Saints, 10 Piazza Pio XII, Rome, Italy, enclosing a copy of the Hindsight column and the New Covenant article.

"Your Eminence," I began, "let me take this opportunity to request that St. Gabriel Possenti be designated Patron of Handgunners.

"In recent weeks, as the enclosures indicate, there has developed a certain public interest in St. Gabriel and in the incident in which he, relying on a simple but Providential demonstration of his handgun marksmanship, was able to rescue the people of an entire town from the clutches of a score of hoodlums.

"Such a designation would be most welcome here in the United States where tens of millions of law-abiding citizens own firearms, including 50 million handguns. It would be also a further indication of the fact that an instrument, in the hands of a person committed in heart, mind and soul to Almighty God, may be used to bring about practical good here on earth."

When I shared a copy of my letter to His Eminence with Catholic writer Mr. Gary Potter, he featured an account of the matter in his weekly May 21, 1987 Intra Urbem Extraque column in The Wanderer, a weekly national Catholic newspaper published in St. Paul, Minnesota.

"Ten years ago," began Mr. Potter, "the Family Live Bureau of the USCC/NCCB (United States Catholic Conference/National Conference of Catholic Bishops) stitched a piece of anti-firearms propaganda onto its annual Respect Life program, producing a preliminary design of the item later peddled by purveyors of fashionable religion as the 'seamless garment.' This is not irrelevant to the story of St.Gabriel Possenti."

Recounting briefly the story of St. Gabriel Possenti, Mr. Potter noted that, "a suggestion has lately been made that he additionally be made patron of handgun marksmen and collectors. The author of the suggestion, advanced in a May 1st letter to the Sacred Congregation for the Causes of Saints in Rome, is John M.

Snyder, chief lobbyist and director of publications and public affairs for the Citizens Committee for the Right to Keep and Bear Arms, an organization that numbers 130 U.S. senators and representatives among its congressional advisors.

"Snyder, a former seminarian and practicing Catholic, is not frivolous. If acted upon, his proposal would go a ways toward helping to counteract the effete pretense and pernicious nonsense that there is never a time for men to take a stand and, if necessary, fight."

After not having had any response from church officials regarding my request, I wrote again, on February 27, 1989, to His Eminence, to "renew my request."

"For your information and convenience," I wrote, "I am enclosing a copy of my original letter of request, along with copies of material published since that time which relate to this matter.

"Also enclosed is a copy of a recently produced prayer card which is relevant to this request."

On April 6, 1989, an official of the Roman Curia, Most Reverend Virgilio Noe, Titular Archbishop of Voncaria, Secretary of the Congregation for Divine Worship and the Discipline of Sacraments, 10 Piazza Pio 10, 00193 Rome, Italy, wrote a letter of response. Possibly this may have been an ecclesiastical bureaucratic version of juggling what was thought to be a sacred hot potato.

He stated that, "the Congregation for the Causes of Saints has forwarded to this Dicastery the request concerning the nomination of St. Gabriel Possenti as Patron of 'Handgunners,'" began the Archbishop.

"May I bring to your attention the norms established by the Holy See with regard to the declaration of a Saint as Patron. The correct procedure is as follows:
1. The election of the Patron by the interested party.
2. The approval of the election by the competent ecclesiastical authority (the bishop for a diocese; the Episcopal Conference for a nation; several Episcopal Conferences for many countries).
3. The confirmation of the Holy See. This can only take place when the above procedure has been followed."

That last statement struck me as rather strange. I thought that the Holy Father, the Pope, known officially in Catholic parlance as the Supreme Pontiff, or, literally, Bridge-Builder, could make such a declaration on his own. After all, why not build a bridge between the official church and the tens of millions of law-abiding men and women throughout the world who own handguns for defense of life?

Chapter 4

What is a Saint?

A Saint is a human being whose heart, mind and will are in conformity with the will of Almighty God for him or her.

God desires that all men, women and children be saints. He wants every human being that ever has existed or ever will exist to be a saint.

God, the Holy Trinity of Father, Son and Holy Spirit, desires this so much that he intervened in human history in a special way. The Second Person of the Trinity, the Son, while remaining God, took on human nature. He, known to history as Jesus Christ, actually was born of a woman, a virgin woman. He actually lived a fully human life. He actually suffered and died. He actually rose from the dead. He did all of this in order to rescue fallen humanity from the grip of the devil. He did all of this to show us human beings how to live a saintly life.

In a basic sense, anyone who lives a life in conformity with the will of God is a saint.

The early Christians believed they had been baptized into the life set forth by the Son, Jesus Christ. They felt they were living this kind of life. They commonly referred to each other as saints. The thinking was that, since all in the church were committed to this life, all were saints.

As the years rolled on, though, certain individuals who had lived and died in an especially saintly manner came to be referred to specifically and distinctly as Saints. Hence, John the Baptist, for instance, was referred to as Saint John the Baptist. Mary, the mother of Jesus Christ, was referred to as the greatest of the Saints. The Apostles were called Saint Peter, Saint Paul, St. Andrew, etc. The Evangelists, that is the authors of the four Gospels: Saint Matthew, Saint Mark, Saint Luke, Saint John. The early martyrs, that is those who died for the faith in Jesus Christ rather than renouncing it before the pagan Roman authorities. Then the confessors. They demonstrated by their lives of outstanding virtue and often by their writings that they lived lives in conformity with the will of God as expressed by the teachings of Jesus Christ and interpreted by the Church that He founded.

The years turned into decades. The decades turned into centuries. The number of members of the Church grew from hundreds to thousands to tens of thousands to hundreds of thousands to millions to tens of millions to hundreds of millions. The external manifestation of the Church, the visible Church, developed a more bureaucratic and hierarchic structure, although the outlines of the structure had been present from the very beginning of the visible Church.

Along with this development came also a more definitive formal use of the word Saint as applied specifically to certain individuals.

In modern times, the formal designation Saint has become reserved for certain individuals. These are men, women and children who have lived lives of outstanding, even heroic, sanctity. The Church has first named them officially Servant of God, then Venerable, then Blessed, then Saint. Ordinarily, for someone to be beatified, or called Blessed, a miracle is attributed to the intercession of the Blessed after the Blessed's death. Ordinarily, for someone to be canonized, or called Saint, an additional such miracle must have been attributed to the intercession of the Saint after the Saint's death. There are strict rules for the acceptance of the authenticity of these miracles. Usually, the miracle involves some physical cure for which competent and authorized medical personnel certify that there is no known natural cause.

By canonizing some of the faithful, that is by solemnly proclaiming that they practiced heroic virtue and lived in fidelity to God's grace, states the Catechism of the Catholic Church, the Church recognizes the power of the Spirit of holiness within her and sustains the hope of believers by proposing the saints to them as models and mediators.

As Rev. Clifford Stevens writes in The One Year Book of Saints, published in 1989 by Our Sunday Visitor, Inc, in Huntington, Indiana, the saints "are those in whom the Christian and Catholic vision has found full growth, who followed the implications of their faith to the fullest degree, and refused to let their lives or their personalities be stunted by the circumstances of the world around them or by the slings and arrows of outrageous fortune."

Father Stevens notes also that while each saint is unique, the saints "are not the exception, since sanctity is the vocation of all." He states that His Holiness Pope Pius XII indicated this diversity and this richness when he wrote that, "One of the merits of Christianity and an indication of its inexhaustible vitality is the fact that the goal which God has set down for everyone, sanctity, can be reached by many different ways. The Spirit breathes how and where He wills, and so we see an immense variety of saints that shine like stars in the firmament of the Church and show the richness of the divine gifts."

Chapter 5

What is a Patron Saint?

According to Webster's dictionary, a patron saint is a saint regarded as the special guardian of a person, group, trade, place, country, etc.

Patron saints, according to Catholic Online, are chosen as special protectors of guardians over areas of life of interest to us. These areas can include occupations, illnesses, churches, countries, causes, anything that is important to us. The earliest records show that people and churches were named after apostles and martyrs as early as the fourth century. Recently, the popes have named patron saints but other individuals or groups can choose patrons. Patron saints today are often chosen because an interest, talent or event in their lives overlaps with the area

There are hundreds of such patron saints. To give the reader just some idea of the variety, these include:
Accountants – Matthew
Actors – Genesius
Advertisers – Bernardine of Siena
Ammunition workers – Elmo
Archers – Sebastian
Armies – Maurice
Arms Dealers – Adrian of Nicomedia

What is a Patron Saint?

Artillery gunners – Barbara
Authors – Francis de Sales
Bankers – Bernardino of Feltre
Booksellers – John of God
Building trade – Stephen
Cattle breeders – Mark
Cavalry – Martin of Tours
Chemists (pharmacists) – Cosmas and Damian
Civil servants – Thomas More
Coin collectors – Eligius
Condemned criminals – Dismas
Dairy workers – Bridgid of Ireland
Dancers – Vitus
Embroiders – Parasceva
Engineers – Ferdinand III
Farm workers – Benedict
Farmers – Isidore the Farmer
Fire fighters – Florian
Fishermen – Andrew, Peter
Fliers and flight crew – Mary, Our Lady of Loreto
Garment workers – Homobonus
Gas station workers – Eloi
Goldsmiths – Anastasius
Gravediggers – Joseph of Arimathea
Hotel keepers – Armand
House hunting – Joseph
Hunters – Hubert
Immigrants – Francis Xavier Cabrini
Infantry – Martin of Tours
Jewelers – Eligius
Journalists – Francis de Sales

Judges/jurists – Ivo of Kermartin
Laborers – James the Greater
Librarians – Jerome, Catherine of Alexandria
Maids – Zita
Metalworkers – Elegius
Miners – Anne (Mother of Mary)
Notaries – Luke, Mark
Ordnancemen and cannoneers – Barbara
Painters – Fra Angelico
Paratroopers – Michael the Archangel
Pawnbrokers – Nicholas of Myra
Pilots – Mary, Our Lady of Loreto
Police officers – Michael the Archangel
Politicians – Thomas More
Postal workers – Gabriel the Archangel
Printers – Augustine
Radio and radio workers – Gabriel the Archangel
Scientists – Albert the Great
Security forces – Michael the Archangel
Senior citizens – Mary, Our Lady of Consolation
Spas – John the Baptist
Swimmers – Adjutor
Swordsmiths – Maurice
Tax collectors – Matthew
Taxi drivers – Fiacre
Teachers – Gregory the Great
Undertakers – Dismas
Venereal disease – Fiacre
Waiters, waitresses – Martha
Writers – Frances de Sales

Chapter 6

Why a Patron Saint for Handgunners?

Why not?

From the preceding chapter, we see that there are patrons for all kinds of things. There are patrons for cannoneers, ammunition workers, arms merchants, hunters, sword manufacturers, politicians, teachers, paratroopers, advertisers, lawyers, doctors, specific disease sufferers and dozens of other activities, professions and interests.

The Church recognizes holy men and women outstanding in various ways by designating them patrons or patronesses of these various activities. Law-abiding handgun owners, and there are tens of millions of us in the United States alone, and probably scores of millions of us throughout the world, also should have a specific patron. After all, people use handguns millions of times each year in the United States alone to defend innocent life or to thwart the perpetration of criminal acts.

By naming St. Gabriel Possenti officially the Patron of Handgunners, the Vatican could hold up this holy man as an example of the proper use of handguns. This would underscore the good purposes to which these inanimate objects can be and often are put. With perhaps hundreds of millions of handguns in the possession of private citizens throughout the world, it behooves the Church to hold up a sterling example of the good way these firearms can and should be used.

It also would call the attention of scores of millions of handgun owners throughout the world to St. Gabriel Possenti. This would lead to a greater awareness of his life and activity. It would lead many to examine his holiness as well as his marksmanship. For the souls of many, it could be a most significant apostolic gesture.

On February 28, 2002, the day after the Feast Day of St. Gabriel Possenti, the Cybercast News Service asked its internet readers, "Is it appropriate to designate a Patron Saint for Handgun Owners?" Of those responding, 63 percent said "yes" and 37 percent said "no."

In recent years, it is true, handguns, handgun ownership, handgun laws and handgun use have become topics of ongoing controversy. It is necessary, though, to keep the facts underlying the controversy in proper perspective.

Perhaps, for one thing, people in general, including some church officials, are not aware of just how many decent people own handguns. If this is the case, they would not comprehend just how beneficial from an apostolic perspective naming an official Patron of Handgunners could be.

In the United States alone today, there easily could be as many as 90 million handguns in the possession of 45 million civilians!

That's adult civilians.

According to the United States Catholic Conference, there are about 65 million baptized Catholics in the United States. This figure includes infants, children and adolescents as well as adults. According to the United States Census Bureau, 70 percent of the people in the United States are adults, that is, 21 years of age or more, the same age as one must be to legally purchase a handgun in the United States. If the 70 percent figure is the same for the Catholic population as it is for the general population, there are about 45.5 million adult Catholics in the United States. That is similar to the number of handgun owners in the United States. Actually, according to the United States Catholic Conference, the percentage of Catholics who are adults may be lower than the percentage of the general population that is adult since Catholics tend to have larger families than does the general population.

In 1997, five years before the writing of the current volume, Aldine de Gruyter of New York published a book on Targeting Guns by Professor Gary Kleck of the School of Criminology and Criminal Justice at Florida State University. A noted scholar in the field, Professor Kleck concluded by that time that there could be as many as 84 million handguns in private possession in the United States. He indicated that each handgun owner, on average, probably possessed two handguns. One could have concluded that by that time there probably were about 42 million handgun owners.

Five years have elapsed since publication of Targeting Guns. During that time, according to Andrew

Molchan, Director of the Professional Gun Retailers Association and the National Association of Federally Licensed Firearms Dealers, handgun production for private consumption in the United States has continued at an average rate of 1,800,000 per year, the same average rate of production for the past 25 years. It seems reasonable to infer, then, that private handgun possession in the United States has reached at least the 90 million handguns/45 million handgun possessors mark.

Regardless of the particulars, though, which may be of specific concern primarily to statistically-oriented scholars, the fact remains that there are a lot of handguns in the possession of a lot of handgun owners in the United States. Worldwide, there likely are scores of millions of handguns in the possession of tens of millions of private citizens.

It is more difficult to obtain detailed estimates regarding the number of handguns in civilian hands throughout the world. According to the Small Arms Survey 2002, a Project of the Graduate Institute of International Studies in Geneva, Switzerland, published by the Oxford University Press in Great Britain, "civilian owners have at least 378 million firearms." This figure includes rifles and shotguns as well as handguns. Today, there probably are at least scores of millions of handguns owned by at least tens of millions of civilians throughout the world.

Why shouldn't we have an official Patron Saint?

Some people may object that handguns are an instrument of murder and other crime and therefore, a

Why a Patron Saint for Handgunners? 23

Saint should not be named as a Patron of Handgunners.

These people, however, would be missing the point completely. A Patron Saint is held up as an example to be emulated. When St. Michael the Archangel is held up as Patron of Paratroopers, this is not to sanction the Nazi paratroop invasion of Greece during World War II. When St. Thomas More was named Patron of Politicians by His Holiness Pope John Paul II, the Holy Father was not sanctioning political activity by the likes of Saddam Hussein, Idi Amin, Adolf Hitler and Joseph Stalin. No way!

Besides, as handgun possession statistics and FBI Uniform Crime Reports indicate, 89,983,000 handguns, or 99.98 percent of the handguns in private hands are not involved in murderous activity in a given year. About 17,000, or one-tenth of one percent, are.

Of the handguns in private possession in a year, 89,972,000, or 99.96 percent, are not involved in deaths related to the overall misuse of handguns. About 28,000, or three-tenths of one percent, are.

According to Professor Kleck, under even a very generous set of assumptions outlined by criminological statisticians, at most 6.7 percent of handguns sold in a given year would ever be involved in even one crime.

This means that with this "very generous set of assumptions," 83,970,000 handguns, or 93.3 percent of the existing handguns, would not be involved in even a single crime. At most, 6,030,000 would be.

Again according to Professor Kleck, under a more plausible set of assumptions, less than two percent of the handguns sold in a given year would ever be involved in even one crime.

This means that with this "more plausible set of assumptions," 88,200,000 handguns, or 98 percent of the existing handguns, would not be involved in even a single crime. About 1,800,000 would be.

Another factor relative to the discussion is the number of times people actually use handguns to defend life, to interrupt crime, or to thwart crime before formal commencement thereof.

After all, on that day in 1860 when St. Gabriel Possenti rescued the villagers of Isola del Gran Sasso, this is precisely what he did. He used handguns to defend life and to interrupt crime. Criminal terrorism, in fact, in that historic case.

According to Professor Kleck, writing in Armed, a book published by Prometheus Books in New York in 2001, there are about 1,900,000 defensive gun uses (DGU) specifically of handguns in the United States per year. That means there are 1,883,000 more handgun DGUs per year than there are homicides committed with handguns. In other words, there are 112 times more DGUs with handguns per year than there are murders per year with handguns.

When one considers non-fatal handgun crime, or crimes committed in which handguns were used but which did not result in death, one notes that there are about 881,000 per year, or 1,019,000 fewer than the number of handgun DGUs per year. In other words, there are about 2.15 times more handgun DGUs than non-fatal handgun crimes per year.

Generally, writes Professor Kleck, "only 24 percent of the gun defenders reported firing the gun, and only eight percent reported wounding an adversary."

Typical of handgun DGU, apparently, is the case of my good friend the late Richard R. Atkinson, Jr., the first treasurer of the St. Gabriel Possenti Society, Inc., and a former Director of the National Rifle Association of America.

At one time, "Rimsky" told me some years ago, a "suspicious" character knocked on his Capitol Hill house door in Washington, D.C. Rimsky answered the knock but kept the chain on the door as he spoke to the knocker. The knocker asked if he could come into the house to use the telephone. Suspecting the possibility of intended foul play, Rimsky replied, "just a minute," and proceeded from behind the door to cock one of his semiautomatic handguns. When the knocker heard the sound of the barrel sliding into position, he immediately ran down the front steps and hightailed it down the street. That confirmed Rimsky's suspicions.

Incidents such as this rarely, if ever, make it into police reports and then into official statistical accounts. They show up only as private accounts and sometime in estimates, statistically, of defensive gun uses.

There are hundreds, if not thousands, of other incidents that do show us each year in newspaper and magazine and other media reports.

One such incident occurred in January of 2002 when Peter Odighizuwa, a 43-year old naturalized citizen from Nigeria, allegedly shot and killed L.

Anthony Sutin, Dean of the Appalachian School of Law in Grundy, Virginia, Professor Thomas Blackwell and another student, Angela Dales, 33. Odighizuwa reportedly had been dismissed from the law school because of failing grades.

When the shots rang out, student Tracy K. Bridges was in a classroom waiting for class to start. A fellow student, Mikael Gross, was outside and just returning from lunch. Utter chaos erupted.

Bridges and Gross immediately ran to their cars and got their guns. Along with Ted Besen, who was unarmed, they approached the gunman from different sides.

"I aimed my gun at him," said Bridges, "and Peter tossed his gun down. Ted approached Peter and Peter hit Ted in the jaw. Ted pushed him back and we all rushed on."

People use handguns for defense of life and property tens of thousands of times each year in the United States. Many, if not most, of these incidents never make it into news reports, or even into police reports. A good number of these cases are similar to the one involving my late good friend Rimsky Atkinson, which never made it into the newspapers. Statistically, though, they show up in surveys regarding the use of firearms for defensive purposes.

A great number of these incidents, on the other hand, do make it into news reports. For several decades now, the American Rifleman magazine, an official monthly journal of the National Rifle Association of America, has featured a regular Armed Citizen page. This feature

Why a Patron Saint for Handgunners? 27

recounts several incidents each month in which law-abiding citizens have used firearms, very often handguns to defend themselves or their families against violent criminals or to thwart the perpetration of criminal acts in progress. These Armed Citizen accounts come from the pages of American newspapers.

In the June, 2002 issue of the magazine, for instance, there appeared an account gleaned from the pages of the Boston Globe, Boston, Massachusetts for March 19, 2002. The report noted that, "an Arlington, Massachusetts, woman shot an intruder after he continued to advance on her when she pointed a gun at him and told him to leave her home. Police said the woman heard one of her dogs barking, retrieved her handgun and went toward her front door. There she saw a strange man standing inside her house. The woman warned him three times, but he said he would not leave, continuing to advance and threatening her. The woman later told police the man moved a hand toward his belt as if going for a gun, so she shot him. 'This guy advanced even after he saw the gun, and that's the sign of an irrational person, or someone who doesn't have your best interest in mind,' said John Serson of the Arlington Police."

Another account in the same issue of the magazine came from the pages of the Kansas City Star, Kansas City, Missouri for April 5, 2002. According to it, "a Kansas City, Missouri burglar's career was cut short when he was confronted by an armed citizen. A Jackson County, Missouri homeowner heard noises coming from his basement one Wednesday morning. He pulled a .38-caliber revolver from under his bed and went to see what was causing the noise. He discovered an intruder in his kitchen and asked him what he was doing there. The man raised his hands, and the homeowner, thinking the intruder had a gun in his left hand, shot him. The would-be burglar staggered to the door and collapsed. The homeowner then saw another man outside his house get into a blue car and drive off. Police later found the car and the burglar's accomplice. Records show the two planned to rob the home and stayed in contact by using walkie-talkies."

In 1998, Cumberland House Publishing, Inc. of Nashville, Tennessee, produced a book written by Robert A. Walters, called The Best Defense, True Stories of Intended Victims Who Defended Themselves with a Firearm.

Mr. Walters is a former director of adult programs for an association of retarded adults and former counselor in the departments of vocational rehabilitation in Tennessee and Florida now living in Ocala, Florida. His book is a collection of human-interest stories of people who used firearms, again, often handguns, to defend themselves or others from violent perpetrators. "The vast majority of these confrontations do not end in violence," he writes, "usually a potential victim merely shows a gun and an aggressor retreats, as happened in the case of Denver's notorious 'Ski Mask Rapist.'

"Since the summer of 1985, this unknown rapist had been terrorizing the city. His method of operation was to stalk single women, determine the nights they would be home alone, and break into their homes after they had gone to bed. He always wore a ski mask and gloves, and cut their outside telephone lines. Once the attacker had isolated his victim, he would brutally rape her, often for hours. The police were stumped as to his identity.

"On January 4, 1986, all had gone according to plan for the rapist. He stood over the bed of his intended victim, erotic fantasies playing in his mind. Rape quickly became an afterthought, however, when the victim suddenly sat up and pointed a pistol between his eyes. The intruder dove through the kitchen window. Investigating officers found that, as in the other cases, the telephone lines had been cut. It took two years, but a task force finally captured Frank Vargas. During that time, the Ski Mask Rapist had violated 20 women. He had been thwarted once, by an armed woman."

Another way of considering the socially beneficial effect of handgun ownership by law-abiding citizens is by looking at the effects of state laws which mandate the issuance of permits to carry concealed handguns to persons who meet certain criteria. Economist John R. Lott, Jr. has spent a lot of time and energy researching just this subject.

As early as August 28, 1996, Professor Lott wrote in The Wall Street Journal "I recently completed a study of one type of gun control law – laws on concealed handguns, also known as 'shall issue' laws. Thirty-one states give their citizens the right to carry concealed handguns if they do not have a criminal record or a history of significant mental illness. My study, with

David Mustard, a graduate student in economics at the University of Chicago, analyzed the FBI's crime statistics for all 3,054 American counties from 1997 to 1992.

"Our findings are dramatic. Our most conservative estimates show that by adopting shall-issue laws, States reduced murders by 8.5 percent, rapes by five percent, aggravated assaults by seven percent and robbery by three percent. If those States that did not permit concealed handguns in 1992 had permitted them back then, citizens would have been spared approximately 1,570 murders, 4,177 rapes, 60,000 aggravated assaults and 12,000 robberies. To put it even more simply: Criminals, we found, respond rationally to deterrence threats.

"The benefits of concealed handguns are not limited to just those who carry them or use them in self-defense. The very fact that these weapons are concealed keep criminals uncertain as to whether a potential victim will be able to defend himself with lethal force. The possibility that anyone might be carrying a gun makes attacking everyone less attractive; unarmed citizens in effect 'free-ride' on their pistol-packing fellows."

As of the writing of the current volume, the number of right to carry states has increased to 32.

The University of Chicago Press published the Second Edition of Professor Lott's book, More Guns Less Crime, Understanding Crime and Gun Control Laws, in 2000. A Senior Research Scholar at the School of Law at Yale University, he wrote that, "98 percent of the time that people use guns defensively, they merely have to brandish a weapon to break off an attack."

He wrote also that, "the empirical work provides strong evidence that concealed-handgun laws reduce violent crime and that higher arrest rates deter all types of crime. The results confirm what law-enforcement officials have said – that nondiscretionary laws cause a greatest change in the number of permits issued for concealed handguns in the most populous, urbanized counties. This provides additional support for the claim that the greatest declines in crime rates are related to the greatest increases in concealed-handgun permits. The impact of concealed-handgun laws varies with a county's level of crime, its population and population density, its per capita income, and the percentage of the population that is black. Despite the opposition to these laws in large, urban, densely populated areas, those are the areas that benefit the most from the laws. Minorities and women tend to be the ones with the most to gain from being allowed to protect themselves."

Sometimes, good people wish they had had a gun for protection when the law prevented them from legally having one.

An unfortunate, classic illustration of this fact occurred on October 16, 1991. On that day, Suzanna Gratia of Copperas Cove, Texas and her parents were customers in Luby's cafeteria in Killeen, Texas. A homicidal maniac, George Hennard, bulldozed his truck through a window and began firing into the crowd of about 150 diners.

Suzanna reached into her purse to get her handgun. Then she realized her handgun was in her automobile because Texas state law at the time prohibited law-abiding citizens from carrying handguns legally for personal protection.

Minutes later, her parents were fatally shot, leaving Suzanna to grieve that she had lost her chance to defend them and the 20 others killed in the melee.

On numerous occasions during the massacre the killer had his back turned to Suzanna, even pausing to reload. Helpless, she could only watch as people, including her parents, were murdered.

"If I'd had my gun, it sure would've changed the odds, wouldn't it," Dr. Gratia, a chiropractor, said at the time.

She still maintains the worst mistake she ever made in her life was leaving her gun in her car in order to comply with Texas law against carrying concealed firearms.

In 1995, however, with Suzanna's goading, the Texas State Legislature passed a bill permitting qualified private citizens to carry concealed firearms.

Gov. George W. Bush signed the bill into law in the spring of 1995. In 1994, Bush ran against an incumbent governor who had previously vetoed a similar measure.

Suzanna, since married, is now Texas State Sen. Suzanna Gratia Hupp!

Her story certainly illustrates, in an unfortunately negative way, the obvious social benefits that may result when handguns are in the hands of good people.

It shows also the absolute stupidity of public policies that prevent this.

Supposing St. Gabriel Possenti had been unable or unwilling to take the bull by the horns on that day in 1860 and confront those renegades in Isola del Gran Sasso with those revolvers? Chances are the marauders would have continued unabated in their marauding. His courageous action demonstrates the good purposes to which handguns can be put. He really ought to be named, formally and officially, the Patron of Handgunners.

In 2001, the National Association of Chiefs of Police (NACOP) asked 23,113 Chiefs of Police and Sheriffs in the United States if they agreed that a national concealed handgun permit would reduce rates of violent crime as recent studies in some states already have indicated. In the 12.0 percent response, 62.3 percent did agree.

It's obvious that the Vatican should designate officially a Patron of Handgunners.

Whether we look at the phenomenon of handgun ownership statistically or from an anecdotal standpoint, it is obvious that handguns, in the hands of good people, can be, and often are, used for good social purposes. In fact, they are used more often for good purposes than they are for wicked purposes.

It's past time for the Vatican to get off the dime, to get on the stick, and to get moving.

St. Gabriel Possenti, pray for us!

Chapter 7

Why Designate St. Gabriel Possenti the Patron of Handgunners?

Again, why not.

His actions on that day in 1860 demonstrate obviously why he should be the choice.

He used a handgun to rescue an entire village full of peaceful, law-abiding people from the grip of a renegade band of soldier/terrorists. He accomplished his mission without causing physical harm, let alone bloodshed, to anyone. He performed his heroic feat after he had entered religious life and had committed himself formally to lead a holy life

St. Gabriel Possenti truly is a holy handgun hero. There just is no doubt about it. He definitely should get the nod. Hopefully, the bureaucrats in the Vatican will see the light.

Besides, St. Gabriel Possenti was known in his young life as a marksman, a marksman with a rifle and a shotgun as well as a handgun, according to Rev. Godfrey Poage, C. P., in his biography of Possenti, Son of the Passion, published by Bruce of Milwaukee in 1962.

Possenti was a holy gunman and he ought to be recognized as such. This would inspire other gunmen and gunwomen to try to cooperate with God's grace and lead holy lives.

Possenti was not only a handgun marksman; he was an heroic handgun marksman. He put his handgun marksmanship to the courageous and charitable service of others when he strode into that village of Isola del Gran Sasso in 1860 and proceeded, alone, to rescue those poor, innocent people from the hands of those cutthroats.

When young Possenti pulled the trigger on that handgun in 1860, he not only defended a village against a band of brigands. He also aimed a bullet at the heart of tyranny, at the heart of terrorism, at the heart of a brute ideology that justifies the use of armed force against the rights of the innocent. He fired a shot at the heart of a burgeoning radical totalitarianism.

Although St. Gabriel Possenti died nearly a century and a half ago, in 1862, and although he was canonized by Pope Benedict XV in the last century, in 1920, he is very much a saint for our times. The terrorists are still very much with us, perhaps now more than at any previous time in our history. Radical totalitarianism is still with us. It presents itself today as a false globalism that would deny the right to life itself; that would prevent people from protecting their own lives and the lives of their loved ones; that would prevent people from keeping and bearing arms for their own protection and for the protection of their loved ones; and that would do all this under the rubric of empowerment of the people!

Today, individuals and nations face the threat of a specific modern terrorism. This is the threat presented by a particularly virulent form of violent, murderous islamism. The world needs a holy modern example of the personal use of force and the instruments of force to repel terrorists and terrorism. St. Gabriel Possenti is the obvious exemplar. Let us pray to him for protection against this modern form of islamist terrorism. Let us hold him up as an exemplar of the proper use of force, of the instruments of force, of handguns, against modern islamist terrorism.

St. Gabriel Possenti truly is a saint for our times. In this day and age, the Catholic Church is in the forefront of the struggle to preserve the right to life. St. Gabriel Possenti shows us that concomitant with this struggle is the struggle to preserve the right to defend life, of the right to the use of the means necessary for the protection of life, of the right to the individual use of firearms, of handguns, for the protection of life.

The Catholic Church, as a genuine and consistent defender of the right to life, also could speak out for the right of the individual to self-defense, of the right to the means necessary for self-defense, of the right to keep and bear arms. As Our Lord and Savior Jesus Christ Himself stated, according to St. Luke's Gospel, "The man without a sword must sell his cloak and buy one."

As a good step in this direction, the Church could declare St. Gabriel Possenti the Patron of Handgunners! In making this gesture, the Church could find hundreds of millions of people throughout the world recognizing it as a courageous institution. Courageous enough to validate the selfless use of force in the defense of the innocent. Courageous enough to stick its neck out for the right of individuals to defend themselves against evil and tyranny. Courageous enough consistently to be not afraid!

Chapter 8

Some Negative Reaction

After I initially petitioned the Vatican in 1987 to formally designate St. Gabriel Possenti the Patron of Handgunners, subsequently renewed my petition in 1989, and attempted to inform the public generally regarding my petitioning activity, international media publicized the activity.

The Associated Press, United Press International, The New York Times, The Washington Post, the Chicago Tribune, the London Times, La Stampa of Turin, Italy, Allegmeine Zeitung of Frankfurt, Germany, even Playboy magazine, for instance, ran articles on my endeavor, as well as did hundreds of other print media outlets.

Typical of the headline coverage of the endeavor was a Washington Post headline on an August 22, 1987 article, which announced, "Handgunners Ask Vatican for Patron Saint." According to the report, Possenti " 'was sort of a holy John Wayne,' Snyder said Tuesday. 'His story would really make a good movie.' "

The London Times headlined its July 24, 1987 report, "Gun lobby raises its sights and seeks a saint." Reporter Michael Binyon reported I told him that naming St. Gabriel Possenti the Patron of Handgunners would indicate the fact that "an instrument, in the hands of a person committed in heart, mind and soul to Almighty God, may be used to bring about practical good here on Earth."

There was considerable radio and television coverage of the endeavor as well.

Radio-TV Interview Report for September, 1987, and Newsmaker Interviews for October, 1987 carried articles about my endeavor and informed radio and TV personnel how they could contact me for interviews on St. Gabriel Possenti, and on my campaign for his official Vatican designation as Patron of Handgunners.

My efforts, however, did not sit well with at least some of the more outspoken Passionists, who objected strongly to them.

Mark Pattison of the Catholic News Service reported on this development. According to his article which appeared in the February 20, 1992 issue of The Catholic Sun of Phoenix, Arizona, "the heads of the two Passionist provinces in the United States have strongly protested efforts to have a Passionist priest declared the Patron Saint of Handgunners.

"Passionist Fathers Robert Joerger and Michael J. Stengle said no evidence exists that St. Gabriel Possenti saved an Italian village from being plundered because of his proficiency in handgun use.

"'Without even getting into the matter of gun control, we are against the proposal on the sheer lack of historical evidence for the incident,' the priests said in a February 4 letter to Archbishop Daniel E. Pilarczyk of Cincinnati, President of the U.S. Bishops' Conference . . .

"'One biographer does mention the incident,' the Passionist provincials wrote in their letter. But 'there seems to be no historical evidence supporting the biographer.'

"The biographer, a Passionist priest, said he is sticking to his story. Fr. Godfrey Poage, a hospital chaplain in California, told CNS February 10 that the superiors 'didn't have the evidence. They didn't see it.' Fr. Poage said the episode was witnessed by a 'lay helper' at the monastery. The documentation was uncovered during his research in Italy in 1947-48."

Later, another Passionist priest, Father Sebastian McDonald, superior of a Passionist monastery, near Detroit, told Mr. Edward Mulholland of the National Catholic Register, according to an article in the publication's March 5-11, 2000 issue, that Father Poage is "an Irishman with a tremendous imagination, and a reputation for story-telling. Things he recounts as facts sometimes end up 60 percent true."

Father McDonald did hedge a little, though, and may have let the cat out of the bag with regard to the real reason some of the Passionists object to naming St. Gabriel Possenti the Patron of Handgunners. Mr. Mulholland reported that, "Father McDonald said the designation as Patron of Handgunners 'would be misleading.' Even if the lizard slaying did occur, it would be taking an incident in Possenti's life and politicizing it, and with a highly charged issue.

"Snyder counters that the politicization comes from

the other side: 'They are more concerned with being politically correct, than they are with being historically accurate . . .'"

In my opinion, it is absolutely amazing, and really disconcerting, that priests would attempt so to impugn the integrity of one of their respected confreres in this manner.

After all, Father Poage had been a peritus, or expert, at the Second Vatican Council. In his biography of St. Gabriel Possenti, Son of the Passion, Father Poage wrote in the Introduction that, "in the final editing this extensive research was summarized. In several places it was necessary to enliven the account with dialogue, but where this was done every word was first checked against the sworn testimony of witnesses in the processes. Nothing was said that had not been quoted by eyewitnesses, at least in the third person."

The clerical attack on the integrity of Father Poage is an absolute outrage.

It is most interesting to me, to say the least, that the attack on Father Poage, and the public questioning of the historicity of the 1860 "lizard incident" did not occur, to the best of my knowledge, until after I petitioned the Vatican to name St. Gabriel Possenti the Patron of Handgunners.

The book by Father Poage was published in 1962 and republished in 1977. Ms. Ann Ball's summary of the account was published in her book on Modern Saints, Their Lives and Faces, in 1983.

Father Poage's book carried the nihil obstat of Frederick Sucher, C.P., S.T.D., Censor for the Congregation of the Passion (the Passionists), the imprimi potest of Walter Kaelin, C.P., Provincial of the Passionist Holy Cross Province, dated February 27, 1962, the nihil obstat of John F. Murphy, S.T.D., Censor librorum, and the imprimatur of Most Reverend William E. Cousins, Archbishop of Milwaukee, dated April 13, 1962

The Ball book carried the nihil obstat of Rev. Joseph Barta, C.M., Censor Deputatus, and the imprimatur of Most Reverend John L. Morkovsky, S.T.D., Bishop of Galveston-Houston, dated August 6, 1980.

The assault on Father Poage's accuracy with regard to the "lizard incident," I repeat for emphasis, did not begin to occur until sometime after I cited it in my campaign for the official Vatican designation of St. Gabriel Possenti as Patron of Handgunners.

Father Poage, however, may already have had the last laugh on those employing outrageous smear tactics. When he died on June 25, 2001, the Passionist Family Circle Newsletter, in its Fall/Winter 2001 issue, stated that he was "a man of extraordinary talents and great kindness," and "a trusted servant of God."

For more than two decades, a quarter century, at least, to the best of my knowledge, the Passionists did not question the authenticity of the "lizard incident." Again, for emphasis, and to the best of my knowledge, some of them began to question the account of it only after I cited it in my petitions to the Vatican and only after the media began publicizing my petitioning activity.

This makes me wonder what in the world is going on with these characters.

Some Negative Reaction

Perhaps they really are more interested in being "politically correct" than they are in being historically accurate.

Perhaps they simply can't bear the thought that one of their Saints actually used force, physical force, to repel an aggressor. There is an unfortunate sense of false pacifism prevalent today among some Christians, some Catholics, some clergymen, and some religious communities. There is a sense that "turning the other cheek" means be a patsy all of the time for anybody and everybody.

That certainly is not genuine Christianity. Let us remember that Our Lord and Savior Jesus Christ, who told us to "turn the other cheek," to more or less ignore certain slights and insults, also counseled His Apostles at the Last Supper that, according to the Gospel of St. Luke, "the man without a sword must sell his cloak and buy one."

Perhaps some of the Passionists want to cover up the "lizard incident." Maybe it is an embarrassment to some of them, to those who prefer pacifism to the muscular Christianity projected by St. Gabriel Possenti in the rescue of Isola del Gran Sasso.

In 1999, when my wife, Ling, and I visited the Shrine of St. Gabriel Possenti in Isola del Gran Sasso, Italy, twice, we shopped for items in the adjacent gift shop. Interestingly, in the books we examined, we found no mention of the "lizard incident." In fact, we found no reference in any of the books we examined to anything about St. Gabriel Possenti for the entire year 1860, the year in which the incident occurred, although one of the books did contain a reference to the book by Father Poage. It appears that any reference to anything during the entire year in St. Gabriel Possenti's life has been eliminated from official literature.

Curious, to say the least.

Cover-up? Could be, in my opinion.

Outrageous? Obviously!

Stupid, too, we believe.

If some of these formally religious people would get their heads out of the sand, in my opinion, and promote St. Gabriel Possenti as Patron of Handgunners, they just might see their vocational program swell with positive responses from truly strong and manly young candidates. That is, of course, if they truly are seeking responses from such candidates.

A statement by Rev. Jack Douglas, Rector of the Passionist Immaculate Conception Monastery in Jamaica, New York, in the Toledo, Ohio Blade of June 29, 2002 makes me wonder. He said that St. Gabriel Possenti "was a very kind, gentle student and associating him with handguns is really something I don't think our community would want." As if an individual could not be kind and gentle and at the same time strong enough psychologically to use handguns in the defense of the innocent!

How absurd!

Think again, Father, think again.

Our campaign proceeds.

St. Gabriel Possenti, Patron of Handgunners, pray for us!

Chapter 9

Founding the St. Gabriel Possenti Society, Inc.

After I petitioned the Vatican in 1987 to designate St. Gabriel Possenti officially the Patron of Handgunners, much publicity and controversy regarding him and the petition ensued, which publicity has continued since that time.

The publicity and controversy developed and proliferated to so great an extent that a number of my friends and associates advised me to form a non-profit entity devoted to proclaiming St. Gabriel Possenti and the whole concept of self-defense that he exemplified.

Among the people who encouraged me greatly in this direction were Mr. Joseph Patrick Tartaro, President of the Second Amendment Foundation and Executive Editor of The New Gun Week, and Chief Gerald S. Arenberg, Founder and Executive Director of the National Association of Chiefs of Police, the American Federation of Police and Concerned Citizens, and the American Police Hall of Fame and Museum.

Consequently, in 1989, a few of us formed the St. Gabriel Possenti Society, Inc. Incorporated under the laws of the Commonwealth of Virginia, but international in scope, the non-profit Society promotes public recognition of St. Gabriel Possenti. We seek his official Vatican designation as Patron of Handgunners. We promote study and exposition of the historical, philosophical and theological bases for the doctrine of legitimate self-defense.

Although St. Gabriel Possenti is a canonized Roman Catholic Saint, the Society is interdenominational.

Religious denominations generally subscribe in some way to the doctrine of legitimate self-defense. The actions of St. Gabriel Possenti in rescuing villagers of Isola del Gran Sasso in 1860 manifest in a personal and operational manner the principle of legitimate self-defense common to various religious denominations. Men and women of various religious persuasions may cite him as an exemplar of this principle.

Also, the era in which we live often has been and is cited as an ecumenical age. It seems appropriate that men and women of different religious persuasions honor St. Gabriel Possenti. It seems appropriate also that men and women of various religious backgrounds encourage Vatican officials to designate St. Gabriel Possenti officially the Patron of Handgunners.

Since the founding of the St. Gabriel Possenti Society, Inc. in 1989, Mr. Tartaro has been most encouraging in the publicity which the weekly newspaper he edits has afforded the activities of the Society. In addition, he has served as a Society Director since its inception.

Chief Arenberg, who died in 2000, was so enthusiastic regarding the founding of the Society that he designed and produced medals that the Society presents to certain individuals who support the goals of the Society.

The circular medal, about two inches in diameter, features an image of St. Gabriel Possenti flanked by silhouettes of a handgun and a lizard. Surrounding the artistic images is appropriate wording: "St. Gabriel Possenti, Guardian Saint of Marksmen, Defenders of the Faith." The Medal is suspended from a neck ribbon.

Later, as detailed in Chapter 17, an Italian gentleman and his associates designed and produced for the Society special medallions for presentation to certain individuals.

Over the years the Society has presented and continues to present Medals or Medallions and accompanying certificates to a number of worthy individuals, both in the United States and abroad.

Among the law enforcement officials who have received these awards over the years are Corporal Regina Bonny of the Midwest City, Oklahoma Police Department; Sgt. Heriberto (Eddie) Carrattini of the Jersey City, New Jersey Police Department; Sgt. Drew Carter of the Texas Rangers; Officer Michael Desmarteau of the Wichita, Kansas Police Department; Deputy Jason Hendricks of the San Barnardino, California Police Department; Lt. Lee Kellogg of the Broward County, Florida Sheriff's Office; Patrolwoman Stacy F. Lim of the Los Angeles Police Department; Deputy Chief Sam Mangialardi of the Chicago Heights, Illinois Police Department; Chief Dennis Ray Martin, President of the American Police Hall of Fame and Museum; Joanne E. Misko, a former Sister of Mercy who became the first female FBI Agent; Detective Scott Perkins of the Orlando, Florida, Police Department; Chief William Ping of the Sparta, Kentucky Police Department; and Inspector William Scott of the U.S. Marshals Service New York Office.

Among clergymen receiving the Medals or Medallions are Rev. J. Winthrop Brainerd, Pastor of Epiphany Catholic Church in Washington, D. C.; Rev. Albert J. Henkel, Pastor of Holy Ghost Church in Knoxville, Tennessee; Most Rev. Archbishop Custodio Alvim Pereira, Vice President of the Chapter of St. Peter's Basilica, Vatican City; Rev. Godfrey Poage, C.P., author of Son of the Passion, The Story of Gabriel Francis Possenti; Rev. Hal Swiggett, Senior Active Member of the Outdoor Writers Association of America; and Rev. Anthony L. Winfield, Baptist Chaplain at Elmhurst Hospital in New York and author of Self Defense and the Bible.

American public officials who have received the St. Gabriel Possenti Society, Inc. Medal or Medallion include U.S. Sen. Bob Smith of New Hampshire, U. S. Reps. Bob Barr of Georgia, Philip M. Crane of Illinois, Bill McCollum of Florida, Jack Metcalf of Washington and Cliff Stearns of Florida, General Richard B. Myers, USAF, Chairman of the Joint Chiefs of Staff, Frank Duggan, Chairman of the National Mediation Board, Mary Jo Grotenrath, Chief/Fugitive Unit, Office of International Affairs, Criminal Division, U.S. Department of Justice, Maryland State Delegate Carmen Amedori, Texas State Sen. Suzanna Gratia Hupp, and Florida District Judge Ellen J. Morphonios, author of Maximum Morphonios.

A number of citizen activists and spokesmen and spokeswomen, past and present, have received the awards. These include Nicholas R. Beltrante, a consulting detective in Alexandria, Virginia; Kenn Blanchard, President of African American Firearms Education; Dr. James T. Brown, Director of the Texas State Rifle Association; Patrick J. Buchanan, a nationally syndicated columnist; Mario Navarro da Costa, Washington, D. C. Director of the American Society for the Defense of Tradition, Family and Property; Shielah Dawson, Director of Gun Owners of New Hampshire; Lt. Col. Frank Kelly, USMC (Ret.), Founder of Virginia Right to Life; Wayne LaPierre, Executive Vice President of the National Rifle Association of America; Jerrold E. Levine, a New York attorney; Bob Lesmeister, Managing Editor of American Firearms Industry; John R. Lott, Jr., author of More Guns Less Crime; James P. Lucier, Ph.D., Senior Editor, Insight on the News Magazine; Gary Marbutt, President of the Montana Shooting Sports Association; Tanya K. Metaksa, Executive Director of the NRA Institute for Legislative Action; Georgia Nichols, Vice President and General Counsel of Mossberg & Sons, Inc. and President of the American Shooting Sports Council; Joseph A. Oertel, President of Anthony Associates, Inc.; Wayne Anthony Ross of Anchorage, Alaska, Chairman of the NRA Gun Collectors Committee; Michael R. Saporito, Chairman of the American Shooting Sports Council; Kevin Steele, Editor of

Guns & Ammo Magazine; M.C. Wiest, Founder of Gun Craft Sports in Knoxville, Tennessee; and Aaron Zelman, Founder of Jews for the Preservation of Firearms Ownership.

Chapter 10

Shooting Facility Dedicated to St. Gabriel Possenti

On April 27, 1991, Rev. Albert J. Henkel, Pastor of Holy Ghost Catholic Church in Knoxville, Tennessee, blessed the Guncraft Sports, Inc. shooting facility and firearms training center, dedicating it to St. Gabriel Possenti.

Father Henkel, who used holy water in the blessing at 10737 Dutchtown Road in Knoxville, conducted the ceremony with the prior approval of Most Rev. Anthony J. O'Connell, Ordinary of the Diocese of Knoxville.

As Founder/Chairman of the St. Gabriel Possenti Society, Inc., I participated in the ceremony, presenting St. Gabriel Possenti Society Medallions to Father Henkel, and to Mr. M. C. "Red" Wiest, Founder and President of Guncraft.

The three of us also got together the next day after Father Henkel's regular Sunday offering of the Holy Sacrifice of the Mass at the Church.

One of the most unique memories I have of the dedication is that of Father Henkel walking between the rows of firearms on display and casting holy water on the guns. Walking behind the priest was Mr. Darrell

Cooper, Manger of Guncraft, wiping the holy water off the gunstocks in fear that the water, if allowed to dry on the stocks, would ruin their appearance, and undermine their value!

Mr. Wiest, who had opened the facility earlier in 1991, commissioned a special portrait of St. Gabriel Possenti by Oak Ridge, Tennessee artist Clarence Frederick Runtsch for it. He said at the time, "I am not interested in publicity for the business. I am interested in whatever protection we can get from St. Gabriel Possenti. My basic purpose is to safeguard the facility here and our customers."

He noted also that Guncraft Sports provides a variety of retail, practice and training facilities for persons interested in marksmanship.

Mr. Wiest, who died on May 13, 2000 of cancer, had graduated from the University of North Dakota at Grand Forks with a degree in chemical engineering.

In May of 1944, he reported to the Clinton Engineer Works at the Oak Ridge Y - 12 Plant and worked on the Manhattan Project. Like many of his co-workers, he believed that his work on the atomic project had helped bring World War Two to a close and he was proud of it. He remained at Y – 12 for 45 years, with most of that time spent on Defense programs.

In 1947, Mr. Wiest turned his hobby of gunsmithing into the Oak Ridge business. That later became Ridge Guncraft, Inc., and then, ultimately, Guncraft Sports, Inc. He also supported summer camps and youth programs that promoted firearm safety and marksmanship.

He was a founding member of the Smoky Mountain Gun Collectors Association and the Oak Ridge Sportsman Association. His favorite pastimes included skeet shooting and taking hunting trips with his family.

Mr. Wiest's two sons, Bob and Tom, currently operate Guncraft Sports, Inc. At the time of the dedication of the facility to St. Gabriel Possenti, he presented me with a lifetime membership, which I treasure to this day.

Chapter 11

Controversy Surrounding the Dedication

On May 3, 1991, shortly after the ceremony dedicating the Guncraft Sports, Inc. shooting facility to St. Gabriel Possenti, I wrote to Most Rev. Anthony J. O'Connell, Ordinary of the Diocese of Knoxville, and stated that, "this is just a note of thanks for your permitting one of the Diocese of Knoxville priests, Rev. Albert J. Henkel, Pastor of Holy Ghost Church, to bless the Guncraft Sports, Inc. facility last weekend during the dedication of the facility to St. Gabriel Possenti.

"As Founder, Chairman and President of the St. Gabriel Possenti Society, Inc., it would be difficult for me to express too highly my sense of appreciation in this matter. With so many tens of millions of law-abiding firearm owners in the United States, it occurs to me that many of these people who do not already share our Faith may, if they become sufficiently acquainted with St. Gabriel Possenti, be inclined, under the influence of Grace, to examine its content. That certainly is my hope and prayer."

I never received a response from Bishop O'Connell who, in May of 1988, had been appointed the First

Bishop of the new Diocese of Knoxville by His Holiness Pope John Paul II.

Subsequently, Gary Ray O'Guinn of the Religious News Service reported on the dedication of the indoor shooting range in an article that appeared in The Wanderer, a national weekly Catholic newspaper, on June 20, 1991, and in other newspapers. The dedication "would not have happened, said Bishop Anthony J. O'Connell, if he had been aware beforehand of what kind of 'business' was involved in the request for blessing. The Bishop, who is taking a live-and-learn approach to the event, said, 'it was more like an ambush than anything else.

" 'Around here, I'm known as an agitator. The last thing people would conclude is that I'm a lobbyist for the right to keep and bear arms. I'm violently in support of gun control,' he said in a phone interview."

On July 2, 1991, Bishop O'Connell wrote Mr. M.C. Wiest, President of Guncraft Sports, Inc. regarding the dedication. He stated that no issue would have been made of it "were it not for the fact that a gentleman from Washington had chosen to come and prepare eventually a news release which was carried by the wire services and which received publicity in the newspapers in which you sent me copies and many others besides.

"I believe the publicity has been unfortunate for the Catholic Church and certainly it gives mixed messages to our own people, as well as to those in other communities (both those who understand us and wish us well and those who do not understand us and who have a tough time with our beliefs and our practices). Nevertheless, I don't believe that there is much we can do at the present time that would undo what has already been done. Therefore, my proposal at the moment is that we do nothing further. I do not intend to make any public statements regarding the event and I believe that in due course it will pass."

In 1998, His Holiness Pope John Paul II appointed Bishop O'Connell Bishop of the Diocese of Palm Beach, Florida Beach.

In 1999, he was elected to a three-year term (1999-2002) as Chairman of the Committee on Marriage and Family Life of the National Conference of Catholic Bishops.

On March 8, 2002, Ken Thomas of the Associated Press reported from Palm Beach Gardens, Florida that, "a Roman Catholic bishop who admitted molesting a teen-ager 25 years ago submitted his resignation Friday, becoming the highest-ranking clergyman brought down in a wave of allegations touched off by the sex scandal in Boston.

"'I am truly sorry for the pain, hurt, anger and confusion I have caused,' said the Rev. Anthony J. O'Connell, Bishop of the Diocese of Palm Beach. 'I've been loved since I entered this diocese, far more than anyone should be loved.'

"O'Connell, 63, admitted to the allegations leveled by Christopher Dixon, his former student at St. Thomas Aquinas Seminary in Hannibal, Missouri. O'Connell was the rector there at the time.

"Dixon, now 40, said the two touched inappropriately in bed after he sought out O'Connell for counseling. Dixon said the abuse began in 1977, when he was 15, and continued to 1980.

" 'For those who will be angry, I certainly ask, when the time is right, that they pray for my forgiveness,' O'Connell said.

"Asked whether he had been involved with other youngsters, O'Connell said there could be 'one other person of a somewhat similar situation, in a somewhat similar time frame.' He would not elaborate.

"O'Connell offered his resignation to the Pope's top representative in the United States, and Diocese spokesman Sam Barbaro said the final decision would be made by the Vatican.

"No one was available to comment at the papal nuncio in Washington."

According to the Associated Press report, "Bishop Wilton Gregory, President of the U.S. Conference of Catholic Bishops, issued a statement Friday night expressing 'profound sorrow and regret' about O'Connell's wrongdoing.

"He restated the Church's commitment to end abuse by clergy and apologized directly to Dixon."

The AP report noted that, "O'Connell, who has been a priest for 38 years, was Bishop of Knoxville, Tennessee, before coming to Palm Beach in 1999. He succeeded J. Keith Symons, the first U.S. Bishop to resign because of sexual involvement with boys.

"After that scandal, Florida's Bishops began background checks for all clergy, lay employees and volunteers who work with children, elderly and disabled people.

"O'Connell said he failed to tell his superiors about the relationship when he was asked to replace Symons.

" 'It should have come up from myself,' said O'Connell, whose admission was first reported by the St. Louis Post-Dispatch.

"O'Connell's admission came only hours after Florida's Bishops issued a statement calling sexual abuse 'both criminal and sinful' and assuring their 2.2 million followers that the Church has procedures to deal with such allegations."

The Associated Press reported also in the same article that, "David Clohessy, national director of the Survivors Network of Those Abused by Priests in St. Louis, called O'Connell's disclosure 'one more painful reminder that an enormous gap exists between the Church's wonderful, flowery words and its leaders' terrible deeds.'

"Dixon said O'Connell's decision was bittersweet to him.

" 'In some ways I feel good that the truth is out there and he's admitted to it,' he said. 'The bad part is that I know a lot of people are going to be upset. But you know, I had to tell the story.' "

According to the AP article, "the Jefferson City, Missouri Diocese paid Dixon $125,000 in a 1996 settlement, and he promised not to pursue further claims against the Diocese, O'Connell and two other priests. The Diocese did not admit any wrongdoing. The two other priests were the Rev. Manus Daly, who allegedly abused Dixon at the seminary, and the Rev. John Fis-

Controversy Surrounding the Dedication 59

cher, who allegedly began abusing Dixon at a Catholic school when he was 11. Daly was removed from a Marceline, Missouri church this week and Fischer was removed from the priesthood in 1993 after allegations involving other children.

"Dixon said he thought he could trust O'Connell when he told him about the abuse from Fischer.

" 'But under the guise of trying to help me come to terms with my own body, he ultimately took me to bed with him,' Dixon said."

On March 14, 2002, United Press International reported from West Palm Beach, Florida that, "the Vatican sent word Wednesday that Pope John Paul II had accepted the resignation of the Roman Catholic Bishop of Palm Beach, Florida. Bishop Anthony J. O'Connell had offered his resignation last week in response to allegations of sex abuse of a seminary student in the 1970s."

On July 29, 2002, Sam Dillon reported in The New York Times from Palm Beach Gardens, Florida that Bishops O'Connell and Symons "kept secret the embezzlement of $400,000."

Bad news, to say the least, right?

You betcha.

This factual history does not in any way establish necessarily that all anti-gun clergymen or all anti-gun bishops are child molesters, but it sure can make one wonder.

Molestation is a perversion, without a doubt.

In my opinion, it also is a perversion, albeit of a different order, to deny decent people the right to self-defense, the right to the means necessary for self-defense.

In any event, a straight shooter such as St. Gabriel Possenti would fight against attempted molestation.

In fact, he demonstrated how he would handle it, showing how an heroic saint reacts to sexual perversion.

He liked to visit his granduncle and had to walk through the "depths of the forest" to do so, according to Rev. Jude Mead, C.P., in his biography, St. Gabriel Possenti, Passionist, A Youthful Gospel Portrait, copyright by L'eco di S. Gabriele in Italy in 1985.

On one occasion, writes Father Mead, St. Gabriel Possenti "was accosted by a young man who first suggested a companionable walk together since he was a stranger. Before he knew what was happening, the stranger tried to lure him into a deserted shack. When it dawned on Gabriel what was happening, he pulled out the hunting knife he carried with him in the woods and exclaimed: 'You fiend! If you try to touch me I'll stick you through.' His tempter fled at once. He was shaking with rage and hurt and did not realize that he still had the knife in his hand when he came upon his friends."

Chapter 12

Fatuous Bishops

It is clear from analyses of statistics on handgun ownership and use that the more handguns there are in the hands of law-abiding citizens the more likely it is that rates of crimes of violence will be reduced. This we demonstrated in a preceding chapter explaining the rationale for seeking official Vatican recognition of a Patron of Handgunners. It also is clear that St. Gabriel Possenti would be most suitable as such a Patron.

Why, then, haven't Catholic Bishops in the United States, proportionately the most handgun-owning country in the world, seen fit to promote this cause?

One potential explanation could be an unfortunately stupid head-in-the-sand attitude towards handgun ownership on the part of at least a large number of American Catholic Bishops.

Without, apparently, examining realistically the facts of the matter, the Committee on Social Development and World Peace of the United States Conference of Catholic Bishops, on September 11, 1975 issued a "call for effective and courageous action to control handguns, leading to their eventual elimination from society." This they proposed in their statement on Handgun Violence: A Threat to Life, without giving due consideration to the fact that handguns are used so many more times to preserve life than they are to threaten life.

In 1978, in the Committee's statement on Community and Crime, they stated, again in typical "our minds are made up, don't confuse use with facts" fashion, a similar position. "We support the development of a coherent national handgun control policy," they stated. Included in that national handgun control policy would be "a several-day cooling-off period between the sale and possession; a ban on 'Saturday Night Specials;' the registration of handguns; the licensing of handgun owners; and more effective controls regulating the manufacture, sale and importation of handguns. We recognize, however, that these individual steps will not completely eliminate the abuse of handguns. We believe that only prohibition of the importation, manufacture, sale, possession and use of handguns (with reasonable exceptions made for the police, military, security guards and pistol clubs where guns would be kept on the premises under secure conditions) will provide a comprehensive response to handgun violence."

Whether these Bishops knew it or not, they were proposing as public policy for the United States, "the land of the free and the home of the brave," a policy similar to that followed by the Union of Soviet Socialist Republics, the state center of international atheistic communism!

Not only that. They're calling for the elimination of handguns, a prime instrument for the defense of innocent life against illegitimate aggression. They also like to ballyhoo how supportive they are of the right to life. How can they profess to be in favor of the right to life at the same time as they seek to eliminate a primary instrument for the defense of innocent life? These people are behaving like total hypocrites.

As recently as 1990, they reiterated their commitment to these idiotic gun-grabbing policies. To the best of this author's knowledge, they have not retreated from that position. Perhaps they're too preoccupied with problems associated with clerical pederasty, including episcopal pederasty.

These Bishops ought to act more like Catholic Bishops and less like slavish followers of every "politically correct" Pied Piper of sociological inanity leading them down the path toward cultural destruction!

They should start paying more attention to the truly great philosophical and theological giants of the Church's tradition. They should restudy, or study, if they have not previously studied in their seminary training, the works of such writers as the Angelic Doctor, St. Thomas Aquinas. If they did, they might develop a proper respect for the real courage and the real charity that St. Gabriel Possenti displayed when he wielded those two handguns against the would-be terrorist destroyers of Isola del Gran Sasso!

St. Thomas Aquinas tackled the question of the legitimacy of self-defense in his Summa Theologica. He did this in a discussion regarding the legitimacy of using force sufficient to actually kill an aggressor if the situation necessitated that.

St. Thomas recalled that, according to Exodus 22:2,

"if a thief be found breaking into a house or undermining it, and be wounded so as to die, he that slew him shall not be guilty of blood." He then comments that, "it is much more lawful to defend one's life than one's house. Therefore neither is a man guilty of murder if he kill another in defense of his own life."

According to St. Thomas, "if a man, in self-defense, uses more than necessary violence, it will be unlawful: whereas if he repel force with moderation his defense will be lawful, because according to the jurists (Cap. Significasti. De Homicid. volunt. vel casual.), 'it is lawful to repel force by force, provided one does not exceed the limits of a blameless defense.' Nor is it necessary for salvation that a man omit the act of moderate self-defense in order to avoid killing the other man, since one is bound to take more care of one's life than of another's."

St. Gabriel Possenti's handgun-wielding rescue of the villagers of Isola del Gran Sasso falls well within the parameters of the thomistic doctrine. After all, he did not even injure physically any of the aggressors. He repelled the aggressors with a clear demonstration of the ability and determination to use force along with the obvious presence in his hands of the instruments of force, the two revolvers.

The American Bishops, though, apparently ignoring both St. Thomas Aquinas and St. Gabriel Possenti, have not seen fit as of yet to take up the handgun patronage cause of St. Gabriel Possenti.

If only they had eyes to see and ears to hear, they might come to realize that, by taking up that cause,

"The Shot"

The Shrine memorializing St. Gabriel Possenti in a Basilica dedicated to him in Isola del Gran Sasso. The waxen image in the glass coffin is carried in processions on special religious days.

St. Gabriel Possenti

Basilica in Isola del Gran Sasso honoring St. Gabriel Possenti

Nave of the Basilica in Isola del Gran Sasso featuring the main altar and artist's conception over the altar of St. Gabriel Possenti's soul ascending into heaven.

M.C. Wiest, Founder of Guncraft Sports in Knoxville, Tennessee, Rev. Albert J. Henkel, Pastor of Holy Ghost Roman Catholic Church in Knoxville, and John Michael Snyder gathered in front of the Church after Mass following dedication of Guncraft to St. Gabriel Possenti.

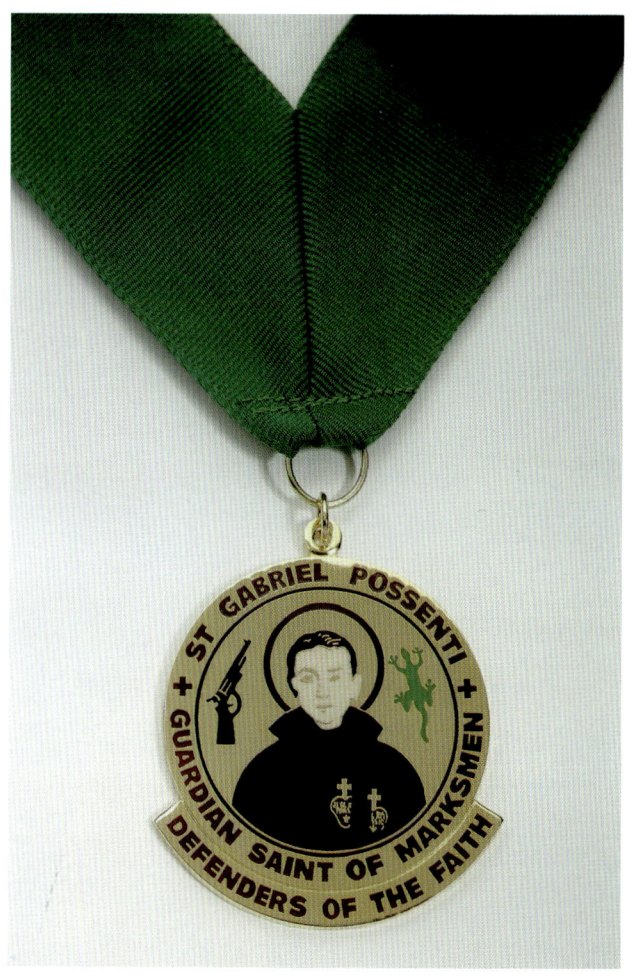

St. Gabriel Possenti Society Medal

> To John Michael Snyder, Chairman and Founder of the St. Gabriel Possenti Society, on the occasion of my enrollment, September 29, 1992, as a pledge of my esteem, with every best wish and blessing.
>
> Father Godfrey Poage, C.P.

Inscription hand written by Rev. Godfrey Poage, C.P. to John Michael Snyder upon Father Poage's presentation of a copy of Son of the Passion to Snyder.

Rev. Godfrey Poage, C.P. presents a copy of his book, Son of the Passion, a biography of St. Gabriel Possenti, to John Michael Snyder in Los Angeles, California.

Archbishop Custodio Alvim Pereira, Vice President of the Chapter of St. Peter's Basilica in Vatican City, accepted a St. Gabriel Possenti Society Medal from John Michael Snyder and wore it next to his pectoral cross during a reception in suburban Washington, D. C.

Years later, Snyder introduced Archbishop Pereira to Francesco Possenti, a great grand nephew of St. Gabriel Possenti, at a conference in Rome, Italy.

St. Gabriel Possenti Society Medallion

St. Gabriel Possenti Society, Inc.

PO Box 2844, Arlington, VA 22202 USA (703) 418-4480 john0849@aol.com

March 5, 2001

Your Holiness John Paul II
Papal Palace
00120 Vatican City State
Europe

Your Holiness:

As the Founder and Chairman of the international, interdenominational St. Gabriel Possenti Society, Inc., I am delighted to present this special medallion to Your Holiness. As a Roman Catholic, I honor Your Holiness for the great achievements on behalf of our Church during Your Holiness' Papacy. When Your Holiness, in the early days of Your Holiness' Papacy, greeted people from the balcony of St. Matthew's Cathedral rectory in Washington, D.C., I was one of the many people in that gathering.

We of this society devote ourselves to St. Gabriel Possenti for particular reasons. As a young marksman with rifle, shotgun and handgun, St. Gabriel Possenti offers us all a holy example of the proper use of these instruments. In the United States alone, over 80 million law-abiding citizens own over 200 million of these firearms. There are many organizations, including a number of Boy Scout troops, which train citizens in their safe and efficient use.

We devote ourselves most particularly to St. Gabriel Possenti because his life shows us the intimate and consistent connection between the right to life, the right to self-defense, the right to the means necessary for self-defense, and the right to arms for self-defense.

Recently, in Rome, on February 27, 2001, the Feast Day of St. Gabriel Possenti, I presented similar medallions to Francesco Possenti, the Saint's great-grandnephew, Most Reverend Archbishop Custodio Alvim Pereira, Vice President of the Chapter of St. Peter's Basilica, Paolo Tagini, Editor of Armi magazine, and other distinguished gentlemen.

Enclosed is a recent article by Mr. Tagini on St. Possenti.

Most respectfully in Our Lord,

John Michael Snyder
Founder/Chairman

enclosure

Letter from John Michael Snyder of the St. Gabriel Possenti Society, Inc. to Pope John Paul II presenting the Medallion to His Holiness

SECRETARIAT OF STATE

FIRST SECTION · GENERAL AFFAIRS

From the Vatican, March 12, 2001

Dear Mr. Snyder,

I am writing at the direction of His Holiness Pope John Paul II to acknowledge your letter and the medal of Saint Gabriel of the Sorrowful Mother that you offered for his acceptance.

I have the honor to assure you of His Holiness's appreciation of the devoted sentiments which prompted this presentation.

Sincerely yours,

Monsignor Pedro López Quintana
Assessor

Mr. John Michael Snyder
P.O. Box 2844
Arlington, VA 22202

The Vatican response to Snyder's letter informing him of the papal acceptance of the Medallion and thanking him for it.

General Richard B. Myers, USAF,
Chairman of the Joint Chiefs of Staff

Rev. Cirilo Nacorda, St. Peter's Church, Lamitan, Basilan Island, Philippine Islands. The photo was obtained with difficulty from the Philippine Islands through the efforts of Mercedes Tira Andrei of the Washington, D. C. Bureau of the Philippine News Agency.

St. Gabriel Possenti Society, Inc. Token.

they could, with the help of Divine Grace, begin to dig themselves out of the pit of stupidity and scandal into which they have dug themselves. The stupidity, that is, of an idiotic policy toward private handgun ownership on the part of law-abiding citizens. And the scandal, that is, of priestly pederasty. After all, as we've seen in a previous chapter, St. Gabriel Possenti, the handgun-wielding Savior of Isola, called one male who wanted to have unnatural sexual relations with him a "fiend," and threatened to stab the guy with his hunting knife!

St. Gabriel Possenti, please ask Our Lord and Savior Jesus Christ to send us some Bishops with guts and common sense!

Chapter 13

A Good Bishop

On January 23, 1999, Mr. Mario Navarro da Costa, Washington Director of the American Society for the Defense of Tradition, Family and Property (TFP), invited my wife Ling and me to attend a reception TFP was holding to honor the Most Rev. Custodio Alvim Pereira, Archbishop Emeritus of Lorenzo Marques, Mozambique.

Msgr. Pereira came originally from Portugal. He had been the Ordinary of the Diocese of Lorenzo Marques in Mozambique. His Holiness Pope Paul VI ordered Msgr. Pereira out of that country. His Holiness had issued the order to protect the life of Msgr. Pereira during a period of violent Communist upheaval in Mozambique.

Msgr. Pereira settled in Rome, Italy. He became Vice President of the Chapter of St. Peter's Basilica in Vatican City.

Mr. da Costa is a Brazilian and thus fluent in Portuguese as well as a number of other languages, including English. At the time of the reception, which followed by a few days the Archbishop's participation in the annual March for Life in Washington, D. C., Mr. da Costa and I had been friends for a number of years.

A Good Bishop

My wife and I appreciated deeply Mr. da Costa's invitation to meet so distinguished a Prelate of the Roman Catholic Church as Msgr. Pereira.

Ling and I were about to leave our residence to depart for the TFP reception. Before closing our door on the way out, I decided to put in my jacket pocket a St. Gabriel Possenti Society Medal. This was one of the medals, suspended from a neck ribbon, that Chief Gerald S. Arenberg, Founder of the National Association of Chiefs of Police, had so generously provided the Society.

In my mind, there was just an off chance that I would be able to present the Medal to the Archbishop.

When Ling and I arrived at the TFP reception, I informed Mr. da Costa that I had the Medal in my pocket. I informed him that, if appropriate, I would like to present the medal to the Archbishop. Mr. da Costa said it might be appropriate to present it to him but that it might not be appropriate to put it over his official hierarchical garments. Mr. da Costa volunteered to ask the Archbishop, in Portuguese, regarding the matter.

Archbishop Pereira spoke in Portuguese to me. Mr. da Costa acted as interpreter.

Archbishop Pereira said he recently had visited the Shrine of St. Gabriel Possenti in Isola del Gran Sasso. He said he would accept the Medal with gratitude.

He not only accepted it. He proceeded immediately to put in on around his neck. Thus, it hung right next to his pectoral cross, an item worn on the breast as a designation of ecclesiastical office.

Ling then took a picture of Archbishop Pereira and me. In the photograph, the Archbishop appears in full ecclesiastical garb complete with pectoral cross and St. Gabriel Possenti Society Medal!

Even prior to the January 23, 1999 reception, Mr. da Costa and the TFP over the years had been most supportive of my efforts to promote official Vatican designation of St. Gabriel Possenti as Patron of Handgunners.

In 1991, in fact, TFP carried a full-page article in the Vol. 5, No. 9 issue of its Newsletter, headlined, "Saint Gabriel Possenti Proposed As Patron of Handgun Owners."

The Saint, ran the article, "was involved in an amazing rescue that should provoke the interest of any competent storyteller. Movie catalogues list dozens of movies where an idealistic handful of men save a small town from a gang of drunken soldiers or rapacious thieves. None, however, could compare with the heroic activities of one determined monk, and for this reason Saint Gabriel's courage and facility with weapons has attracted the attention of John Snyder of Arlington, Virginia, who is proposing the saint as patron of handgun owners."

The article outlined the life of St. Gabriel Possenti, describing in some detail his rescuing the villagers of Isola del Gran Sasso.

"What better choice could John Snyder . . . have made," concluded the article. "Saint Gabriel magnificently combined deep piety and a selfless, heroic defense of the order God placed in the universe that is so rarely evident today."

Chapter 14

A Good Christian Minister

St. Gabriel Possenti's 1860 pistol-wielding rescue of the Isolan innocents exemplifies a principle common to a number of religious persuasions. That is the doctrine of legitimate self-defense, of the right to use force to repel the use of force against the innocent.

It is true that there are a number of religionists, including clerics, of various faiths, who somehow feel it is a horrible thing ever or practically ever to use force, and certainly handguns as an instrument of force. That kind of thinking, however, really is just the pompous pedantry of pacifistic prune heads. It has no legitimate doctrinal basis.

Rev. Anthony L. Winfield examines this issue from a biblical perspective concisely but thoroughly in his scholarly monograph on Self Defense and the Bible.

Rev. Winfield, a St. Gabriel Possenti Society Medal recipient, has been a hospital chaplain at Elmhurst Hospital in Brooklyn, New York since 1987. He also is a veteran U.S. Marine Corps combat infantryman. He spent a year in Vietnam in the late 1960s with the 1st Marine Division.

In 1985, Rev. Winfield was ordained as a minister of the Gospel at the East End Baptist Church of Brooklyn in fellowship with the Conservative Baptist Association of America. This followed conferral of a B.A. in Psychology from the Empire State College of New York, a Masters Degree in Religious Education from Gordon-Conwell Theological Seminary, and a Masters of Divinity Degree from the New York Theological Seminary.

In the preface to his monograph, which the St. Gabriel Possenti Society, Inc. distributes, Rev. Winfield writes that, "during my journey as a Christian I received theological training and moved into positions of leadership in a local church. It didn't take long for me to notice the widespread confusion surrounding the subject of self-defense. A common misconception was that the Bible prohibited Christians from bearing arms for self-defense. The popular teaching of 'turning the other cheek' was used as a proof-text to discourage Christians from even entertaining the thought that the use of deadly force was allowed – even when one's life or that of a loved one was threatened by a dangerous criminal.

"Though I at first ignored this trend, the accelerating violence both here and abroad moved me to carefully examine the Bible in order to put to rest the naivete and distortion about the use of deadly force by devout men and women of God. My sentiment was that if 'self preservation is indeed the first law of nature' then in reality the instinct to survive is a God-given one. If so, then the Bible – as the Christian's blueprint for life – must contain some clear evidence supporting the right to bear arms for self-defense. Surely the Almighty would want his servants to know for sure . . .

"In short this brief study aims to prove that God does not forbid His servants from bearing arms for self-defense if he/she chooses to. That even Christ instructed his disciples to buy and bear arms. That even the 'turning the other cheek' doctrine upon close examination does not forbid self-defense. And that the major arguments opposing self-defense can be easily refuted."

In his summary of his Old Testament study, Rev. Winfield asserts that, "over and over again we saw how God did indeed approve of His children using deadly force under certain circumstances. And that the only act of deadly force condemned by God as a sin was the unjustified slaying of an innocent human being. Engaging in the rescue and the protection of innocent loved ones and property, and the waging of holy wars, were sanctioned by God. There's no question that the testimony of Scripture reveals that God instilled in His people the idea that it was better to be armed than unarmed."

Rev. Winfield analyzes certain New Testament texts and rephrases them in a modern context.

At the Last Supper, for instance, according to the Gospel of St.Luke (36:22), Our Lord and Savior Jesus Christ clearly told his disciples that, "the man without a sword must sell his cloak and buy one."

Rev. Winfield notes that the statement, in today's usage, would read, "he that has no handgun, let him sell his coat and buy one."

Rev. Winfield notes also that, "the new 'turn the

other cheek' doctrine was in essence teaching Christians not to seek revenge for an injury or an offense at the hands of a foe. It taught restraint! Moreover, a slap in the face has been universally accepted in all cultures as an assault on one's pride – not a threat to one's life! Does anyone really believe that 'turning the other cheek' means that a devout Christian woman must submit to a rapist? No one in his/her right mind would answer in the affirmative. And what if the woman decided to defend herself by grabbing a frying pan to bash the criminal's head in, does that make her a 'bad' Christian? Does anyone really believe that a 'good' Christian should allow himself/herself or a loved one to be maimed or killed by a criminal? Is there any biblical evidence that God's people allowed themselves – because they were morally obliged to – to be killed by evildoers without resistance?"

Chapter 15

Armed Catholic Nuns

On July 21, 1999, two cloistered Roman Catholic nuns in central Colombia shot and killed a thief who broke into the Sanctuary of the Virgin of Miracles at the El Tobo convent in Tunja, about 80 miles northeast of Bogota, the country's capital.

The nuns, Sister Eva Maria Silva, and Sister Luz Adelia Barragan, a convent administrator, each fired the .38-caliber Smith & Wesson revolver at the intruder, Severo Mendez.

Sister Barragan fired three shots. Sister Silva then took the handgun and emptied the cylinder in the direction of the intruder.

During the incident, Mendez was hit twice, once in the head and once in the hand.

Earlier in the year, the 25 nuns at the sanctuary began night-time patrols. They did this because of seven previous break-ins. Chickens and some religious relics were stolen during these break-ins.

Subsequently, the nuns were arrested, charged with murder, and jailed for two days before being released on bail.

For Sister Silva, the court hearing was the first contact with the outside world since 1970. Sister Barragan, because she is a convent administrator, reported the Associated Press, had been permitted to leave the monastery. AP reported that the shootings attracted national attention. Fed up with rampant violent crime rates, the wire service indicated, many Colombians said they sympathized with the nuns' actions.

"By their action," I stated in a news release issued July 26 on behalf of the St. Gabriel Possenti Society, "these two religious nuns demonstrated clearly that handguns can be used for good purposes of self-defense and defense of property. This incident shows also that, without the handgun, the terrified sisters could not have protected themselves and the other 23 nuns in the convent from physical harm and robbery. The nuns bought the handgun in 1981 following a series of attempted robberies. After six break-ins this year, they started nightly patrols.

"Even though the good sisters are understandably upset that the vicious intruder died as a result of the incident, this should serve as a warning to the criminal element that religious persons and establishments are not necessarily easy targets. Nuns, too, have a God-given right to self-defense. These nuns acted truly in the spirit of St. Gabriel Possenti, who used a handgun to defend innocent victims against violent criminal acts."

The release prompted a telephone call and international interview with Colombian public radio, which translated my words of support for the two sisters into Spanish.

On August 4, the charges against the nuns were

dropped. The public prosecutor's office released a statement confirming that "the nuns acted in self-defense."

Subsequently, I sent Sister Barragan and Sister Silva each a St. Gabriel Possenti Society Medal and Certificate.

Chapter 16

Genocide

One of the great crimes of the Twentieth Century, if not the greatest crime, was the crime of genocide, the oft-repeated attempt on the part of governments to eliminate entire civilian populations.

Most people, including most people in public life, generally condemn genocide.

However, a number of the same people also promote various forms of restrictive gun control.

This is difficult to understand.

They seek to make it legally difficult if not impossible for private citizens to obtain firearms, especially handguns. Many seek to eliminate the private possession of firearms, especially handguns. They seek to use government authority to disarm the people living under the jurisdiction of the government.

This dual position essentially is a mutual contradiction.

Government commits genocide.

People who do not have guns are not able effectively to resist genocide.

People who support restrictive forms of gun control making possible the disarmament of the people in reality support policies that, if implemented, make it impossible for people to resist genocide.

Unfortunately, even a number of church officials of various religious persuasions maintain this mutually contradictory attitude. They oppose or even condemn genocide on the one hand but, on the other hand, support the gun control policies that make possible the implementation of genocidal policies.

Such people, including the schizoid religious types, obviously do not manifest the spirit of St. Gabriel Possenti, who used handguns to rescue the people from the grip of renegade soldiers.

One gentleman who clearly has demonstrated the connection between certain public gun control policies and genocide in a detailed, scholarly manner is Mr. Aaron Zelman, a holder of a St. Gabriel Possenti Society Medal.

Mr. Zelman is the Founder and Executive Director of Jews for the Preservation of Firearms Ownership.

He and Mr. Richard W. Stevens are the authors of a book on Death by Gun Control, published by Mazel Freedom Press of Hartford, Wisconsin.

In a chapter on Roman Catholicism and Self-Defense, and a section therein on The Patron Saint of Handgunners, they recount the 1860 lizard incident. They write that, "Gabriel Possenti was canonized later for other reasons, but the St. Gabriel Possenti Society has been promoting him as 'the Patron Saint of Handgunners,' and has asked the Vatican to make it official."

In their book on Death by Gun Control, Messrs. Zelman and Stevens show that each of the genocides of the Twentieth Century was preceded by government confiscation of privately held firearms. Each confiscation itself had been preceded by the enactment of restrictive firearm laws making possible the confiscation policy.

This is a most serious work. It demonstrates that Twentieth Century governments murdered 170,000,000 people. That is 170 million people. One hundred seventy million people.

Government, history's supreme mass-murdering entity, perpetrated the horror of repetitive genocide by first disarming the people. They did this after implementing gun control policies that made possible the genocide.

Messrs. Zelman and Stevens maintain that Hatred plus Government plus Disarmed Civilians equals Genocide.

Among the genocidal governments they list are Ottoman Turkey, 1915-1917, 1 – 1.5 million Armenian (mostly Christian) victims; the Soviet Union, 1929-1945, 20 million political and farming community victims; Nazi Germany and Occupied Europe, 1933-1945, 20 million political opponent, Jewish, Gypsy, critic, "example" victims; Nationalist China, 1927-1949, 10 million political opponent, army conscript and other victims; Red China, 1949-1952, 1957-1960, 1966-1976, 20-35 million political opponent, rural population, enemies of the state victims; Guatemala, 1960-1981, 100,000-200,000 Mayans and other Indian and political enemy victims; Uganda, 1971-1979, Christian and political enemy victims; Cambodia (Khmer Rouge) 1975-1979, educated person and political enemy victims; and Rwanda, 1994, 800,000 Tutsi people victims.

The factual history is one of tyranny and horror. Brutal horror. All made possible by certain gun control policies – policies that America's Founding Fathers precluded through the Second Amendment to the U.S. Constitution.

The good, holy, charitable, courageous, manly St. Gabriel Possenti, wielding the two handguns against the evildoers, is an actual symbol of resistance to tyranny. And of the horrors which tyranny perpetrates.

St. Gabriel Possenti, pray for us! Pray that the Holy Spirit so send forth His light and His strength into the hearts and minds of the responsible officials of the Roman Catholic Church that they have the wisdom, prudence and fortitude to designate you officially the Patron of Handgunners!

Chapter 17

Visiting Isola del Gran Sasso

In November of 1999, my wife Ling and I, during a vacation in Italy, on two separate occasions visited the village of Isola del Gran Sasso and the Shrine there of St. Gabriel Possenti.

Isola del Gran Sasso, which means, literally, Island of the Great Rock, is about a three-hour drive from Rome.

The drive is a scenic one from Rome and the outskirts of Rome through some plains and up into the Apennine mountain range. Isola is a village of not more than a few hundred people situated within sight of the "Great Rock" mountain. It is not too long a drive from there to the coast of the Adriatic Sea.

On the drive from Rome to Isola, we passed by Aquila, a fairly large town about one hour's drive before coming to Isola. In the winter, it is a favorite ski resort.

The village of Isola would seem to appear much as it did during the time of St.Gabriel Possenti, with the obvious major exception of paved roads. Most of the buildings appear to have been there for many generations.

Ling and I walked up and down several of the narrow streets of the village, taking quite a few pictures during our two visits.

The Shrine of St.Gabriel Possenti is adjacent to the village. It is located within a Basilica that lies in front of the Passionist Monastery where St.Gabriel Possenti lived the last years of his life and where he died.

According to literature available at the site, when St. Francis of Assisi arrived there in 1215, he found at the location a chapel dedicated to the Annunciation of the Blessed Virgin Mary. In 1216, construction began nearby for a monastery and a larger church dedicated to the Immaculate Conception of Our Lady.

Restored in 1590, the church was enlarged in 1908 to its present size for the Beatification of St.Gabriel Possenti. It was embellished by the addition of the dome in 1920 for the canonization of St.Gabriel Possenti and in 1929 it was further adorned by the elegant façade.

The simple, traditional exterior of the Basilica features a number of columns supporting a second-story façade displaying frescoes of the vocation, or religious calling, of St. Gabriel Possenti, of the death of St. Gabriel Possenti, and of St. Gabriel Possenti in heavenly glory.

In the interior, on the right side of the nave is the Chapel of St.Gabriel Possenti that was inaugurated in 1920. Under its altar is a waxen image of St.Gabriel Possenti placed in a glass coffin. In 1920, the mortal remains of St.Gabriel Possenti were enclosed in a metal statue and placed under the altar in a gilded bronze urn.

A number of paintings and sculpted statues may be observed by visitors walking around the interior of the church. Included are a number of paintings of St. Gabriel Possenti in different situations and a bust of Pope Benedict XV, who canonized him in 1920. There is a fresco of St. Gabriel Possenti in Glory in the vault, done by Scaramucci in 1921.

Near a column in the right transept of the Basilica is a small-enclosed area that marks the original tomb of St.Gabriel Possenti. From a nearby office in the Basilica we obtained several packets of material marked "Polveri del Sepolcro di S. Gabriele dell'Addolorata," Gabriel of the Sorrowful Virgin being the religious name taken by our Patron.

Ling and I prayed there and then visited the gift shop upstairs. We purchased several interesting items, including a statue of St. Gabriel Possenti. As indicated in a previous chapter, though, we were quite surprised to find no mention in any of the literature of the 1860 lizard incident or, for that matter, of any events during the year 1860. As indicated in that earlier chapter, the apparent cover up attempt is most disturbing.

A number of religious people, unfortunately, including some clerics, try to promote Christianity and its heroes as limp and pasty, weak, gutless, effeminate, and ineffectual. To such people, two-gun St. Gabriel Possenti must cause many a nightmare. Tough. Let them whine!

Plopped right in front of the elegant Basilica is what I can describe only as an incongruous architectural bomb. It is a huge structure which dwarfs, physically, the Basilica. Construction of this newer church, called the New Sanctuary, began in 1970. In comparison with the Basilica, it's huge. If it was located somewhere else, one might consider it a fine example of modern church architecture. Located where it is, though, it really seems out of place.

During our 1999 visit to Rome, Ling and I were the guests of a triple-crested Italian nobleman, who traces his family history to about 1200, and his wife. They wish to remain anonymous. In the mid-1990s, the Count, a pistol marksman and firearms enthusiast, and himself a devotee of St. Gabriel Possenti, read about my efforts to promote public recognition of St. Gabriel Possenti.

He contacted the National Rifle Association of America and located my address through that organization. He then contacted me and, after a while, we began a correspondence. When I informed him that Ling and I were planning to visit Rome, he extended the invitation to us and we accepted. He and his wife have been most gracious and generous hosts.

During our 1999 visit to Rome, the Count informed me that he would like to make for special distribution by the St. Gabriel Possenti Society, Inc. a limited number of medallions of precious metal featuring a special engraved profile of St.Gabriel Possenti on the obverse. The reverse would feature the name of the Society and a special message and/or the name of the recipient.

He said he intended to have the medallions made

according to the elegant style of mid-nineteenth century papal, royal or military medallions.

The Count asked me if I thought this was an acceptable project. Of course I responded in the affirmative.

After Ling and I returned to the United States, the Count during the following several months sent me several proposed designs for the medallion. After much correspondence back and forth across the Atlantic, we finally agreed on a particular design.

Subsequently, he proceeded to contact Miss Roberta Rubegni, who designed the obverse of the medallion, as well as noted engraver G. Guccione in Rome. The Count has produced a number of these beautiful medallions. The recipients all have felt honored to accept them.

In this project and in a number of other ways as well, the Count has proved himself a true and generous friend of the St. Gabriel Possenti Society, Inc.

Chapter 18

A Call From a Possenti

On February 26, 2000, the eve of the Feast Day of St. Gabriel Possenti, Dr. Francesco Possenti phoned me from Milan, Italy to our home in Northern Virginia.

Needless to say, I was surprised and delighted to receive that call early on a Saturday morning!

Dr. Possenti explained that he is a great grand nephew of St. Gabriel Possenti. He said that he had read recently in two Italian newspapers and had heard recently on Italian television about my efforts to promote official Vatican designation of St. Gabriel Possenti as Patron of Handgunners. He said also that he would like to receive some literature about the St. Gabriel Possenti Society, Inc.

We exchanged several letters. Among the materials he sent me were pages from a history of his family, written in Italian by Rev. Ladislao Ravasi, C.P., showing his relation to St. Gabriel Possenti. Francesco, ironically, was the Saint's name before he took the name Gabriel of the Sorrowful Mother on entering formally the religious state of life.

The current Francesco Possenti, married to the former Daniela Malin, was born in 1940. He is the son of Guido Giovanni Possenti, who was born in 1903, and of his wife, the former Elena Lo Presti. Guido Giovanni Possenti was the son of Francesco Tommaso Possenti, who was born in 1869, and of his wife, formerly Zelinda Piermarini. Francesco Tommaso Possenti was the son of Michele Possenti, who was born in 1834, and of his wife, formerly Mariana Dionisi Vici.

Michele Possenti was a brother of Francesco Possenti, later known as Gabriel Possenti, who was born in 1838.

Michele and Francesco and a number of other siblings were the sons of Sante Possenti and of his wife, formerly Agnese Frisciotti. According to Father Ravasi's history, the couple parented 13 children.

According to a synopsis of St. Gabriel Possenti's life found in a biography by Rev. Gabriele Cingolani, C.P., Saint Gabriel Possenti, Passionist, translated from Italian to English by S. B. Zak and published in New York by the Society of St. Paul in 1997, Possenti was born in Assisi on March 1, 1838, in the municipal building of the Town Square, and baptized in the Cathedral of Saint Rufinus. In April or May, the family moved to Poggio Mirteto, where his father was named governor. In November, the family moved to Spoleto, where his father was named legal assessor of the papal delegation.

On February 9, 1842, Francesco's mother died of meningitis.

In 1844, he began elementary school with the Brothers of the Christian Schools.

On June 1, 1846, Francesco was confirmed in the Church of St. Gregory by the diocesan bishop, Most

Rev. John Sabbioni.

In 1848, his brother Paul died in Choggia.

Two years later, in 1850, he began his secondary school studies at the Jesuit school in Spoleto. The year after that, probably on June 21, he made his First Holy Communion. He was outstanding in humanities studies at school.

In 1853, another brother, Lawrence, 27, committed suicide in Rome.

In was during the 1850s, according to Rev. Godfrey Poage, writing in Son of the Passion, that young Possenti began to acquire a reputation both for dancing ability with young women and for rambunctious behavior outdoors. He is known to have had lots of fun with mixed company but also to have been sort of a local holy terror. One of the things he liked to do was ride a horse up to the front doors of houses, cause the horse to rear up, and smash his front hoofed feet against the front doors! Apparently, this scared the living daylights out of some of the neighbors.

During this period also, according to Father Poage, young Possenti became acquainted with a Major O'Reilly, the newly appointed commandant of the papal fortress of La Rocca. "This soldier of fortune," wrote Father Poage, "had left Ireland in the uprising of 1849, spent some four years training papal troops, and than obtained a commission from Cardinal Antonnelli.

"Major O'Reilly was a capable soldier. He knew how to handle a gun and was well versed in the care and training of cavalry horses. The papal army needed men of his caliber, so Cardinal Antonnelli, the secretary of state under Pope Pius IX, never questioned his background. He accepted the major for what he was, an honest and capable soldier, and gave him command of the garrison at Spoleto...

"O'Reilly liked Spoleto and came to be accepted by the elite of the town. One of the things that helped him socially was his friendship with the Possentis. He took a fancy to Francis and taught him the fine points of riding, showed him how to care for a gun, and let him practice on the rifle range. Francis became so proficient with a firearm that before long he could pick off a bird on the wing.

"Sante was pleased with this new interest and for Christmas that year gave Francis a shotgun."

In 1854, again according to Father Cingolani's synopsis, Possenti recovered from a serious throat illness, the second one, thinking he was miraculously cured. He asked to be admitted by the Jesuits, was accepted, but never entered.

The following year, Possenti's sister, Mary Louisa, died unexpectedly at age 26. Possenti requested copies of his school records, considered a "sure sign" that a decision regarding his future vocation was under way.

In 1856, he received copies of other school records. He received an interior locution during a procession with an image of the Blessed Virgin Mary during which she urged him to become a religious. His confessor Father Charles Bompiani confirmed the authenticity of his religious calling.

He gave a recitation, to a standing ovation, at the Marian school assembly where the academic honors for the Jesuit school in Spoleto were awarded.

He left Spoleto for the Passionist House in Morrovalle, stopping in Loreto along the way, where he had an intense inner experience confirming the vocational decision he had made. He went on a spiritual retreat and entered the Passionists, taking the religious name of Brother Gabriel of Mary, Our Lady of Sorrows.

In 1857, after a year of novitiate, he professed the religious vows of poverty, chastity and obedience as a Passionist.

In 1858, he completed his studies of philosophy and Latin and was transferred to Pievetorina.

In 1859, he began his theological training, and made the trip to Isola del Gran Sasso.

In 1860, according to Father Poage's account, Possenti rescued the villagers of Isola del Gran Sasso with that striking, one-shot, lizard-slaying demonstration of handgun marksmanship.

The following year, 1861, he received tonsure and minor orders as a first formal step to the priesthood, but his health began a rapid decline. He continued to grow worse, couching up blood.

In 1862, on February 27, at 6:30 in the morning, he died of consumption.

In 1891, an official investigation into the life and virtues of Gabriel Possenti was opened by the ecclesiastical authorities at Terni, his father's birthplace. In 1896, Pope Leo XIII authorized the formal introduction of the cause of the canonization of Gabriel Possenti. When it was proved that he had exercised in a heroic degree the theological virtues, he was beatified by Pope Saint Pius X in 1908.

After examining the sworn evidence of over a thousand cases of miracles reported through the intercession of Gabriel Possenti, the Sacred Congregation of Rites determined that two of them were "absolutely incontestable," in the words of Father Poage. One involved John Baptist Cerro, who had been cured instantaneously of severe arthritis. The other involved Aloysius Parisi, who had recovered immediately from a grievous abdominal rupture.

Originally, the canonization date was set for May in 1913. However, the approach of World War One necessitated a delay in the ceremony. The outbreak of hostilities, which began in 1914 and did not terminate until 1918, delayed the ceremony for the entire decade. In May, 1920, Pope Benedict XV finally was able to proclaim Gabriel Francis Possenti among the blessed in heaven, a Saint. There were 45 cardinals, 280 bishops, and 61,000 visitors present for the occasion in Rome.

Among those present for the event was Michele Possenti, a brother of St. Gabriel Possenti, and the great grandfather of my new correspondent from Milan, Francesco Possenti.

Chapter 19

Rome Conference

On February 27, 2001, the Feast Day of St. Gabriel Possenti, the Italian Count, my wife Ling and I hosted a luncheon and conference in commemoration of our Patron in Rome.

For the specific location, we selected the Hotel Columbus, an historic establishment dating actually to the time of Christopher Columbus, and situated within the shadow of St. Peter's Basilica in Vatican City.

During the social hour prior to the luncheon, Ling and I were delighted to actually meet Dr. Francesco Possenti, the great grand nephew of St. Gabriel Possenti, who traveled by train with his wife, Daniela, from Milan to participate in the conference.

It was my great pleasure, too, to introduce the Possentis to Most Rev. Archbishop Custodio Alvim Pereira, Vice President of the Chapter of St. Peter's Basilica. Ling and I had met Archbishop Pereira earlier, in the United States, as explained in the Chapter on A Good Bishop, and he had placed the Possenti Medal suspended from a neck ribbon around his neck so that it fell right next to his Pectoral Cross.

Archbishop Pereira participated in our Rome luncheon through the good offices of Miss Virginia Coda

Nunziante, of the Rome based Lepanto Foundation. She is a true friend and genuine devotee of St. Gabriel Possenti who is fluent in several languages.

Archbishop Pereira said the grace at the luncheon and extended the official blessing of the Catholic Church to the participants. I presented him with one of the personalized boxed Possenti Medallions which had been developed in Rome.

During the luncheon, which happened to fall that year on a Tuesday, the day before Ash Wednesday, Archbishop Pereira told us that he would be offering the evening Mass the following day in St. Peter's Basilica. Ling and I appreciated that information and we did attend that Mass on Ash Wednesday. We received our ashes that year the Italian way, with the ashes sprinkled over the head, rather than the American way, with the ashes placed on the forehead.

During the conference following the luncheon, I presented similar boxed medallions to a few select invitees.

These recipients included Dr. Francesco Possenti as well as a few others.

One of these, Dr. Piero Raggi, is a noted Italian scholar. He is the author of La Nona Crociata, a history of the men who fought on behalf of Blessed Pope Pius IX in defense of the Papal States in the mid-nineteenth century. Dr. Raggi included a description of the "lizard incident" and an item regarding the St. Gabriel Possenti Society, Inc. in his most recent edition, published in 2002.

Another, Mr. Paolo Tagini, is an Editor of Armi, a

most respected and superior Italian firearms periodical. He has written several times about St. Gabriel Possenti and the Society. A great defender and exponent of the traditional right to self-defense, he has been of great assistance in identifying the type of handguns used in the "lizard incident."

Col. Jeff Cooper flew all the way from Paulden, Arizona to accept his medallion. Col. Cooper, who for many years has been well-known within the firearms community, is a genuine war hero who has written a number of books and an untold number of articles on the right to self-defense as well as the technical aspects of firearms development, construction and use. He is the Founder of the Gunsite Ranch, an establishment which provides training in various aspects of defensive combat shooting.

As Master of Ceremonies for the conference, I extended to all present "what we hope and pray will be the first of many such gatherings of our international, interdenominational St. Gabriel Possenti Society. We gather here in the center of Catholicism, in the shadow of the Basilica of St. Peter the Apostle, to commemorate and honor St. Gabriel Possenti, one of the great heroic figures of Church history, on his Feast Day.

"There are many reasons for memorializing St. Gabriel Possenti. Our particular reason is to recall the incident in 1860 when St. Gabriel Possenti rescued the villagers of Isola del Gran Sasso from a gang of terrorists. With great courage and outstanding concern for the safety and welfare of others, St. Gabriel Possenti demonstrated his handgun marksmanship."

After recounting the highlights of the "lizard incident," I offered my belief that, "when young Possenti pulled that trigger, he not only defended a village against a band of brigands. He also aimed a bullet at the heart of tyranny, at the heart of a brute ideology that justifies the use of organized force against the rights of the innocent. He fired a shot at the heart of a burgeoning radical statism.

"Although St. Gabriel Possenti died nearly a century and a half ago, in 1862, and although he was canonized by Pope Benedict XV in the last century, in 1920, he is very much a saint for our times. The terrorists are still very much with us, as a reading of the daily newspapers, or as a viewing of television will readily tell us. Radical statism is still with us, too. It presents itself today as a false globalism that would deny the right to life itself; that would prevent people from protecting their own lives and the lives of their loved ones; that would prevent people from keeping and bearing arms for their own protection and the protection of their loved ones; and that would do all of this under the rubric of empowerment of the people!

"Yes, St. Gabriel Possenti truly is a Saint for our times. In this day and age, the Roman Catholic Church is in the forefront of the struggle to preserve the right to life. St. Gabriel Possenti shows us that concomitant with this struggle is the struggle to preserve the right to defend life, of the right to the use of the means necessary for the protection of life, of the right to the individual use of firearms for the protection of life. The Catholic Church, as a genuine and consistent defender of the right to life, also could speak out for the right of the individual to self-defense, of the right to the means necessary for self-defense, of the right to keep and bear arms. As Our Lord and Savior Jesus Christ Himself stated, according to St. Luke's Gospel, 'The Man without a sword must sell his cloak and buy one!'

"As a good first step in this direction, the Church could declare St. Gabriel Possenti the Patron of Handgunners! In making this gesture, the Church could find hundreds of millions of people throughout the world recognizing it as a courageous institution.

"Courageous enough to validate the selfless use of force in the defense of the innocent.

"Courageous enough to stick its neck out for the right of individuals to defend themselves against evil and tyranny.

"Courageous enough consistently to be not afraid!"

During the conference, one of the reporters present, Ms. Frances D'Emilio of the Rome Bureau of The Associated Press, noted that she earlier had questioned the Vatican press office regarding my campaign. A spokesperson had told her that in the past the press office had noted that naming a patron saint for handgun owners "isn't opportune."

In her account of the conference, that appeared in the United States and elsewhere, Ms. D'Emilio reported that, "Snyder, who said the Vatican told him a few years ago that he needed to enlist bishops around the world for his cause, said he would not be discouraged.

"'I intend to keep bringing this to the Vatican's attention till they finally get the message,' Snyder said at the ceremony. 'Things in the Catholic Church often take a very, very long time.'"

There were a number of interesting comments made during the conference.

One in particular came from Mr. Mario Marcone of Sulmona.

Mr. Marcone noted that there was a certain symbolic interpretation which could be given the "lizard incident." The lizard, he said, could be seen as a miniature representation of a dragon, a symbol of evil, a symbol of the Devil. By slaying the living symbol of evil, St. Gabriel Possenti used the handguns against evil itself!

Among the others who attended the luncheon and conference were some seminarians from the United States who were studying at the North American College in Rome.

One of these young men had seen the web site for the St.Gabriel Possenti Society and had contacted me via e-mail for more information. A hunter and firearms enthusiast himself, he said he expected to be ordained shortly and would be serving parishioners where hunting with firearms, including handguns, was popular. He said he thought his apostolate would be facilitated if he knew more about the shooting saint and could tell his future parishioners about him.

In response, I had told him of our forthcoming conference and invited him to come and to bring with him any of his seminarian associates who might be interested. He and three other fellows showed up. They were all very grateful.

A couple of days after the conference, my wife Ling and I took the seminarian who had contacted me originally to dinner. He suggested that I attempt to present one of the boxed medallions to His Holiness Pope John Paul II. He said I should write a letter to His Holiness with appropriate references and address it to the Holy Father through the Secretary of the Papal Household, Bishop James Harvey, an American. That seminarian even suggested the specific Vatican entrance I should approach and with which Swiss Guard station I should leave the package.

I did just as that seminarian suggested. In my March 5, 2001 letter accompanying the presentation of the Medallion to the Pope, I wrote, "we devote ourselves most particularly to St. Gabriel Possenti because his life shows us the intimate and consistent connection between the right to life, the right to self-defense, the right to the means necessary for self-defense, and the right to arms for self-defense."

In a March 12, 2001 Vatican response, Monsignor Pedro Lopez Quintana, Assessor, wrote "at the direction of His Holiness Pope John Paul II to acknowledge your letter and the medal of St. Gabriel of the Sorrowful Mother that you offered for his acceptance.

"I have the honor to assure you of His Holiness' appreciation of the devoted sentiments which prompted the presentation."

Chapter 20

Send Them a Message

On the Feast Day of St. Gabriel Possenti in 2002, February 27, during a news conference at the National Press Club in Washington, D.C., I unveiled the St. Gabriel Possenti Society tokens.

The one and one-half inch aluminum coins feature an image of St. Gabriel Possenti flanked by silhouettes of a lizard and a handgun on the obverse.

The reverse contains the message, "Support Vatican endorsement of St. Gabriel Possenti as Patron of Handgunners." In includes also the Society's web site address, www.gunsaint.com.

Churchgoers of various persuasions throughout the United States and the world may send church officials a message by depositing the tokens in weekly collection baskets.

The Society distributes quantities of the coins to interested people in the United States and in other countries as well.

With this distribution, we're hoping to foster an international, ecumenical grass-roots movement calling upon the Vatican to designate St. Gabriel the Patron of Handgunners.

One of the reporters who covered the news conference was Jason Pierce of the Cybercast News Service (CNSNews.com).

Mr. Pierce wrote that, "as for using a saint to further a pro-gun point of view, Snyder contends the right to defend one's self is consistent with the right to life.

"'I think that this is part and parcel with the movement to defend life,' Snyder said. 'St. Gabriel Possenti used a handgun to defend an entire village, showing therefore that handguns can be used to preserve life.

"'I believe that any organization that believes in the right to life has got to believe in the right of decent people to use guns to defend themselves and other people,' he said.

"Snyder said that just because his organization is honoring the use of handguns, especially Possenti's use of a gun, it does not mean it supports everyone who uses a gun.

"'There are many who use handguns to do horrible things, but there are those who use handguns to do wonderful things, which happens more often than evil uses of handguns,' Snyder said. 'The way I see it, Saddam Hussein is a politician, but just because we have a patron saint of politicians (St. Thomas More), that doesn't mean we are honoring Saddam Hussein.

"'When the Church sets up a holy person as a patron of some profession or activity, it is showing the good end to which these activities would be put,' Snyder said."

Mr. Pierce also reported that "Desmond Riley, spokesperson for the Coalition to Stop Gun Violence, disagrees with Snyder's reasoning.

"'I would think there are a lot of greater causes to make someone a (patron) saint for things other than handguns,' Riley said. 'I think it is a tenuous stretch, from what this guy did to make him the Patron Saint of Handgunners.'

"When informed of Snyder's proposal, a spokeswoman from the Violence Policy Center gave a terse response: 'No comment.'"

Chapter 21

Presentation to the Chairman of the Joint Chiefs of Staff

On Friday, September 13, 2002, my wife Ling and I met General Richard B. Myers, USAF, Chairman of the United States Joint Chiefs of Staff, during a reception in his honor at the National Press Club in Washington, D. C.

We both told him we supported him in his efforts to lead the 21st century war against international terrorism. He seemed most appreciative of our comments, and was most gracious in his conversation with us.

Ling and I live in an apartment in Northern Virginia, on the southern bank of the Potomac River, which actually overlooks the Pentagon. From our balcony, we also view other structures of national significance, such as the U.S. Capitol, the White House, the Basilica of the National Shrine of the Immaculate Conception, the Washington Monument, the Jefferson Memorial, the Lincoln Memorial, and others.

On the morning of September 9, 2001, we both were home. We heard the crash into the Pentagon of the airliner which islamist terrorists had hijacked. As I later learned, a woman I had known for some years was on the flight and perished in the attack. For days, the sky around us was blackened with the smoke from the crash. Ling even placed towels under our apartment door in an effort to keep out the smell from the crash.

Consequently, we feel some direct connection with the war on international terrorism.

I myself am appalled at the pacifist attitude taken by some individuals in the face of the direct threat our country and the free world face from these militant Islamic fanatics. I am thoroughly disgusted by this attitude on the part of some supposedly religious individuals, including some Catholic prelates.

When Ling and I told General Myers he had our complete support in the war against international terrorism, we really meant it!

It occurred to me that there is some similarity between St. Gabriel Possenti and his single-handed rescue of the villagers of Isola del Gran Sasso from a gang of terrorists in the mid-nineteenth century and General Richard Myers and his attempt to rescue the United States and the world from the international terrorists of the early 21st century.

I thought it appropriate to present General Myers with a St. Gabriel Possenti Society Medallion, of the type designed in Rome. I made that private presentation at the National Press Club, expressing my sentiments to General Myers. He seemed most appreciative.

I think it appropriate, too, that people ask St. Gabriel Possenti to intercede with Our Lord so that General Myers may receive heavenly guidance in his conduct of the war and so that it may be brought to a victorious conclusion.

Presentation to Chairman/Joint Chiefs of Staff 103

Shortly after our meeting with General Myers at the National Press Club, a neighbor of ours who is a U.S. Army officer assigned to the Pentagon, Lt. Col. Herbert "Zak" Grogan, offered to deliver to General Myers a certificate and explanatory letter from me to accompany the Possenti Medallion.

On October 16, 2002, General Myers replied by letter. "Many thanks," he wrote, "for your informative letter forwarding the St. Gabriel Possenti Society certificate to accompany the medal you presented me at the National Press Club in September. I sincerely appreciate the thoughtful gift.

"Your interest in St. Gabriel Possenti is indeed commendable. It is a fascinating story about his life and the subsequent recognition to include the doctrine of self-defense. The medal is a unique addition to my collection . . .

"Again, many thanks for the kind words and thinking of me in this special way. Best wishes for continued success with the Society and for your forthcoming book."

On January 17, 2003, The New York Times reported that Gen. Myers, in October, 2002, approved a government document that "outlines an approach that aims to disrupt and destroy terrorist organizations like Al Queda, and confront countries and organizations that sponsor or support terrorism."

Chapter 22

Rev. Cirilo Nacorda

Rev. Cirilo Nacorda is a contemporary Catholic priest whose experience reflects to a striking degree the experience of St. Gabriel Possenti.

Father Nacorda is a parish priest of St. Peter's Church in Lamitan on Basilan Island in the Philippine Islands.

Basilan Island is one of the areas in the Philippines which in recent years has been subjected to the terrorist activities of the Abu Sayyaf, an extremist islamist group with ties to the international extremist islamist organization Al Queda, according to reports. The predominantly Muslim island province of Basilan, in fact, was the birthplace of Abu Sayyaf, according to the Associated Press.

Father Nacorda himself was a captive of Abu Sayyaf for a period of about two months in 1994. The Philippine government ransomed him for two million pesos, according to the Philippine Inquirer News Service.

The bandit group, led by the late Commander Abdurajak Janjalani, had captured Father Nacorda and 69 others. The Abu Sayyaf took the 70 from Barangay Matarling in Lantawan town. Of that group, "15 were summarily executed while the others were held captive and released allegedly after the payment of ransom," reported the Inquirer News Service.

Father Nacorda "has been caught more than once in the crossfire from the Muslim guerrillas," reports AP, "prompting him to arm himself and organize others to defend Christians on Basilan against the Abu Sayyaf."

The 45-year old Father Nacorda now carries a .45-caliber semiautomatic handgun along with his Holy Bible. He also has a 9mm automatic firearm, according to The Washington Post.

He carries the .45 "for my protection," he states. "The Abu Sayyaf do not respect life, and the military cannot provide 24-hour protection."

He says also that, "we cannot protect ourselves by just prayers or dialogue. We have to be practical."

Father Nacorda has organized a 3,000-member armed group to defend Christians.

Around midnight on June 1, 2001, according to the AP's Jim Gomez, "about 70 Abu Sayyaf guerrillas burst into a small hospital, a nearby church and a convent at the heart of Lamitan's dusty downtown, dragging along their hostages from the distant island resort.

"Lamitan, home to more than 60,000 people thriving on coconut farming and fishing, is especially coveted by the Abu Sayyaf. The town, along with the provincial capital of Isabela, are the only two places dominated by Christians in Basilan.

"Nacorda said he was cornered by two young rebels who pointed their guns at him outside the church at the start of the assault, but he ran away before they could fire.

"The men shot to death Nacorda's driver and a church worker, apparently mistaking one of them for him, yelling 'The priest is dead!'"

When asked about the propriety of a Catholic priest carrying a gun for protection, Father Nacorda says that, "Life is so precious. This is God's gift to us and I have to protect it. I believe God understands my predicament and why I need to do this. He knows my heart."

Father Nacorda, according to Mark Baker, writing in The Age, "has been threatened with death more often than he cares to remember."

The priest says, "I know there are a lot of people who would be happy to see me dead, including members of the military and some of its leaders here. I am afraid, but I have no choice but to speak out."

He says that during the 2001 Abu Sayyaf attack on the hospital in Lamitan guerrilla fighters were allowed to escape after army officers were handed cases containing about 22 million pesos, or about 800,000 American dollars, in cash.

"Our problem is not just the Abu Sayyaf," he says. "Our real problem is the extent of corruption among the military and local government officials."

Meanwhile, according to the Philippine Star, "the Catholic Bishops' Conference of the Philippines (CBCP) expressed support to the call of Fr. Cirilo Nacorda for Basilan residents to arm themselves against the Abu Sayyaf terrorists.

"'I think we can tolerate it as long as its purpose is self-defense. In ordinary circumstances, a priest should not be carrying a gun, but we must understand that a special situation exists in Basilan. It is dangerous (there),' said CBCP spokesman Msgr. Hernando Coronel."

After learning about Father Cirilo Nacorda, I wrote him on June 10, 1992 that, out of respect for the memory of St. Gabriel Possenti, "and for the traditional Catholic doctrine regarding the right to self-defense and the means thereto which he exemplifies and symbolizes, and out of appreciation for the magnificent commitment to these same principles which you have and do demonstrate in your priestly ministry, and for which you have been cited in the international media, we have prepared for you a special sterling silver St. Gabriel Possenti Society Medallion. The Medallion has been designed and struck especially for the Society in Rome, and the reverse has been especially engraved with your name and the date of the Saint's Feast Day this year in the Eternal City.

"Last year in Rome, His Holiness Pope John Paul II, His Excellency Most Rev. Archbishop Custodio Alvim Pereira, Vice President of the Chapter of St. Peter's Basilica, and Mr. Francesco Possenti, great grand-nephew of St. Gabriel Possenti, accepted similar Medallions from our Society.

"We hope you will accept our presentation of this Medallion and await your response."

On July 18, Father Nacorda wrote in response that "I am deeply honored to be a recipient of a sterling silver medallion from your prestigious Society.

"Much as I like to come to receive it personally I have to apologize for not making it. My ministerial job and as a spokesman for my fight for truth and justice takes me away most often to other places from all over the Philippines.

"Going to the States to accept this award is such a great idea but there is my responsibilities to my parishioners. Also, the peace and order situation is not quite normal yet.

"If it is possible that the Medallion can be forwarded or sent to me in Lamitan will truly make me happy and I am deeply grateful to you.

"I do hope, kind Sir, you would understand the predicament I am in.

"Please pray for me, for my life and for all of us, Lamitenos.

"Thank you so much for the honor."

Subsequently, on November 25, 2002, my wife Ling and I visited the Philippine Embassy in Washington, D.C. We met there with Mr. Ariel Y. Abadilla, Deputy Chief of Mission, and Ms. Joy Quintana, Cultural Officer. They agreed to provide for the transmittal of the Medallion to Father Nacorda. I presented it, along with an accompanying certificate and letter of transmittal, to Mr. Abadilla, who was about to visit the Philippines. Later, Ms. Quintana informed me that Mr. Abadilla had presented the Medallion to Philippine personnel in Manila for hand delivery to Father Nacorda.

"We of the Society think you are a great hero," I wrote in my letter of transmittal to Father Nacorda. "We are honored and delighted that you have agreed to accept our token of appreciation for your contributions to the cause of freedom and of the right to self-defense and for your service to the people of God in the Philippine Islands.

"We ask now only that you remember us when you offer the Holy Sacrifice of the Mass."

On January 25, 2003, Ms. Quintana phoned to inform me that the Medallion had been delivered to Father Nacorda in the Philippines on January 17.

Chapter 23

An Age of Peril

We live in an age of peril.

Militant islamist terrorists are on the march throughout the world, determined to undermine and destroy societies based on human freedom and on Judaeo-Christian principles.

This unfortunate fact of contemporary life was brought home in a personal way to my wife, Ling, and me during the September 11, 2001 suicide bomber attacks on the United States.

We live in an apartment on the Virginia side of the Potomac River overlooking the Washington, D. C. skyline and the Pentagon. Pending an appointment, we were both at home when the terrorists struck the Pentagon. The terrorists, who had commandeered a commercial jetliner, flew that plane directly into the Pentagon.

Although we did not actually see the crash, we sure did hear it.

After the crash, black smoke billowed in the neighborhood for days. Ling covered up the space under the door to our apartment with towels to keep out the smoke. Small bits of metal from the crashed airplane actually landed at several points around the building in which we live.

Later, I learned that a woman I had known for several years was on the plane which the terrorists smashed into the Pentagon.

One of Ling's girlhood friends works in that section of the Pentagon which was bombed. Luckily, she had decided just a few days before the atrocious event to take off some vacation time and so was not in the building when it was attacked.

Since that terrible September 11, it really has become clear to all who have eyes to see and ears to hear that our civilization is in a war for survival.

Central to this war for survival, although it is not "politically correct" to say so, is a struggle between those who hold dear the spiritual values of our society and those who abhor, hate and despise those spiritual values.

This war is not simply an economic war or a political war, although it surely is that in part.

At root, it is a spiritual war.

It is a spiritual war with material aspects.

It is a war the successful fighting of which demands both commitment to spiritual principles and facility in the use of material weapons of war.

It is a war which demands, in other words, the same kind of commitment to spiritual principles and the kind of ability and willingness to use force and the instruments of force which St. Gabriel Possenti manifested that day in 1860 when he took up arms, handguns, to rescue the innocent Isolans from the renegade military force terrorists.

By naming St. Gabriel Possenti, officially, the Patron of Handgunners, the Vatican could reassert in a striking manner the traditional principle that the use of force and the instruments of force in defense of life, truth, justice, and innocence against unjustified and nefarious aggression is not only acceptable but sometimes necessary.

In this one fell swoop, too, it could do much to rid the clergy, especially the Catholic clergy, of a reputation for impotence, for ineffectual mamby-pambyism, for an inability to come up with real solutions to real problems.

It could show that there is not a dichotomy between truth and strength but that there is in fact a nexus between them.

Readers who may be wondering what they can do to promote this cause actually can do a lot.

For one thing, you can spread the word by providing copies of this book for your friends, relatives, associates and clergymen of various religious persuasions.

For another thing, you can obtain and distribute copies of the St. Gabriel Possenti "gunsaint" tokens among your friends and associates. A fine way to spread the word and to send church officials a message is by depositing these coins in church collection baskets.

You can write to the recently-named Prefect of the Congregation for Divine Worship, the Vatican office now charged with responsibility for selecting official Patrons for various reasons. You can tell him you believe that St. Gabriel Possenti ought to be named

Patron of Handgunners.

That Prefect, named to his position by Pope John Paul II during the latter part of 2002, is Francis Cardinal Arinze.

The address for the Congregation is Piazza Pio XII, 10; 00193 Vatican City. The telephone number is (011) 39-6-6988-4318. The fax number is (011) 39-6-6988-3499.

Most importantly, though, you can pray, asking Almighty God to inspire the bureaucratic officials of the Church to heed the cry of the faithful for naming St. Gabriel Possenti the Patron of Handgunners!

Appendix A

Prayer from an Anonymous Source

St. Gabriel Possenti, we pray you, who have shown virtue in sacrifice and courage as well as in shooting skills, to give our weapons your blessings, so that they may serve only to defend, and never to bring harm, so that in this life we may find and give friendship and brotherhood.

Guide our aim so that we may strike center with our weapons, and more so with our behavior, to become worthy knights of this age.

Protect us from the enemies of Love, Justice and Liberty, and give us strength to prevail in the struggle. Amen.

Appendix B

Prayer Composed by the Author

Glorious St. Gabriel Possenti, during your life on earth you delivered from danger the innocent victims of public disorder and criminal violence by the courage God gave you, the handgun marksmanship skill with which you were blessed and the presence of firearms in your capable hands at a most providential moment.

May the Most Holy Trinity, through the intercession of the Blessed Virgin Mary, to whom you were so devoted throughout your mortal life, grant that Holy Mother Church formally designate you the Patron Saint of Handgunners in order that everywhere handgunners may have a personal and holy example of the proper, safe and efficient use of handguns.

With your assistance, may we always use our gifts, the exigencies of our lives and even the material creatures with which we come in contact for the genuine good of our neighbor, our own eternal salvation and the greater glory of God Our Father, through Our Lord Jesus Christ, in union with the Holy Spirit, One God, for ever and ever. Amen.

Appendix C

Firearms: The Handgun Saint: Gabriel Possenti

By Jeff John, Firearms Editor
Scope
(Reprinted with permission from the Fall 1999 issue of the Petersen Sportsman's Society Scope, with credit to Primedia)

Saint Gabriel Possenti was born Francis Possenti, the eleventh of 13 children born in Assisi, Italy in 1838 to Sante and Agnes Possenti. An appointed public official, Sante was also a church and government lawyer. The family moved to Spoleto where Francis grew to become a dandy, being nicknamed "the Dude" by his friends, who also styled themselves "The Lords of Spoleto." Francis enjoyed theater, dancing, smoking, cards, gambling and also hunting, becoming an expert marksman with both rifle and shotgun.

During an annual religious procession through Spoleto, Francis was moved to join the Church.

Francis applied and was accepted to the order as a novice. He was given the name Gabriel and began his religious training.

Upon completion of his initial training for the priesthood, Gabriel was sent to the monastery of Isola del Gran Sasso in the Kingdom of Naples. There was much political turmoil at the time and the priests thought that the remote monastery would be a safe place for the young men to continue their studies.

It was not to be so. In 1860, a marauding band of deserters from either Garibaldi's army or Victor Emmanuel's Piedmontese army approached Isola, and most of the people fled to the wilds. The few who stayed behind watched in horror as the unopposed soldiers drank, looted and burned with abandon. The town militia fled without a fight. The rector of the monastery, Father Valentine, locked himself in his room and prayed for salvation. Many of the other priests fled or locked themselves away as well. Gabriel was shocked and dismayed at the cowardice around him. In growing anger he begged permission of the cowardly Father Valentine to help. In town, he found 20 drunken soldiers ransacking and burning. A soldier who was dragging off a young girl confronted the young monk. When the soldier moved close, Gabriel snatched the drunken lout's revolver and threatened to shoot him if he did not unhand the girl. A second soldier arrived and also was disarmed by the forceful monk.

The ruckus brought the rest of the soldiers to the scene. Brandishing a brace of revolvers, Gabriel demanded that the men disarm. Liking the odds, the gang's sergeant dared the lone monk to stop the whole company. When a lizard darted into the street and paused, Gabriel pointed his revolver at it and killed it with one shot.

Cocking and pointing both revolvers at the sergeant,

Gabriel again commanded the men to lay down their arms or he would put the next shot through the sergeant's heart. His impressive marksmanship had unsettled the sergeant, who did not wish to be the first to die. Laying down their arms, the 20 soldiers were unburdened of their loot and bent to the task of quenching the fires they had set. Gabriel then marched the men to the city's limits and set them on the road.

There is a lot in this story that is left unsaid. Much of it probably will never surface, but some of it is worthy of contemplation. For instance, the diminutive St. Gabriel apparently disarmed his opponent very easily. Could it be that the drunken lout had his pistol in a butt forward holster? There is a lesson there, perhaps. Cross-draw holsters present the butt of your gun to your opponent's strong hand. St. Gabriel also chose the sergeant – the one with the loudest mouth – to threaten with death. Courage and a stout heart often can overcome tremendous odds, especially with a little help from Col. Colt. And what kind of guns were they? According to Val Forgett of Navy Arms, the handguns of Garibaldi's army were Italian copies of the Colt 1851 Navy in .36 caliber! Shades of Clint Eastwood.

John Michael Snyder founded the international, interdenominational St. Gabriel Possenti Society, Inc. in 1989 to promote recognition of Possenti, seeking his official Vatican designation as Patron Saint of Handgunners.

The society emphasizes the historical, philosophical and theological bases for the doctrine of legitimate self-defense. It publishes a monograph titled Self

Defense and the Bible by the Rev. Anthony L. Winfield.

The Society Medal features an image of Possenti flanked by silhouettes of a lizard and a handgun surrounded by the legend: St. Gabriel Possenti-Guardian Saint of Marksmen-Defenders of the Faith. A certificate accompanies it.

In a private ceremony on January 23, Snyder, Chairman of the St. Gabriel Possenti Society, Inc., presented the Society Medal to Archbishop Custodio Alvim Pereira, Vice President of the Chapter of St. Peter's Basilica in the Vatican. One of the goals of the society is to receive official recognition from the church for the legitimate use of force in legitimate self-defense. Prior recipients of the society's medal include the Rev. Godfrey Poage, C.P., the Possenti biographer; Rev. Cliff Stearns of Florida; Kevin Steele, group editorial director of the Petersen Outdoor Group; Georgia Nichols, President of the American Shooting Sports Council; and Wayne LaPierre, Executive Vice President of the National Rifle Association.

Contact the St. Gabriel Possenti Society, Inc., P.O. Box 2844, Arlington VA 22202. (703) 418-4480, or through www.gunsaint.com.

Appendix D

Pistol Packin' Piety: A Patron Saint for Handgunners?

By Edward Mulholland
(Reprinted with permission from the March 5-11, 2000 issue of the National Catholic Register)

ARLINGTON, VA – Peruse any list of saints and you will find a patron for almost every occupation and activity.

St. Fiacre is the patron of taxi drivers, even though he lived hundreds of years before the invention of automobiles and yellow cabs (he also appears as patron of hemorrhoid-sufferers).

An organization based in Arlington, Virginia, the St. Gabriel Possenti Society, is petitioning the Vatican to name its saint the patron of handgun users.

St. Gabriel Possenti was a 19th century Passionist. He is already a patron of youth, students and clerics. His feast day is celebrated February 27.

Why the new title?

A 1962 biography of the saint by Passionist Father Godfrey Poage, Son of the Passion: The Story of Gabriel Francis Possenti, recounts an episode in which Gabriel, then a seminarian, rescued the villagers of Isola, Italy, from a gang of some 20 terrorists with a striking, one-shot, lizard-slaying demonstration of handgun marksmanship in 1860.

The St. Gabriel Possenti Society's literature summarizes the story:

"A slim figure in a black cassock stood facing a gang of mercenaries in a small town in Piedmont, Italy. He had just disarmed one of the soldiers who was attacking a young girl, had faced the rest of the band fearlessly, then drove them all out of the village at the point of a gun . . .

"When Garibaldi's mercenaries swept down through Italy ravaging villages, Brother Gabriel showed the kind of man he was by confronting them, astonishing them with his marksmanship, and saving the small village where his monastery was located.

"The mercenaries' leader told the young religious brother that it would take more than just one monk with a handgun to make the mercenaries leave town.

"The future saint pointed out a lizard which was running across the road. He shot the lizard right through the head, at which point the mercenaries decided that discretion was the better part of valor.

"They obeyed the monk's orders to extinguish the fires they had started and to return the property they had stolen. They then fled the village, never to be heard from again."

Possenti died in 1862 and was canonized by Pope Benedict XV in 1920.

The St. Gabriel Possenti Society was founded in 1989 by John Snyder, who works for the Citizens Committee for the Right to Keep and Bear Arms, a pro-gun lobbying group. Snyder told the Register that, after hearing the story of St. Gabriel, he wanted to start an organization "to promote awareness of him and his life, and this incident in particular."

According to Snyder, a Catholic, "For those of us who believe strongly in the legitimacy of the defense of life and property, he personifies this very Catholic and very natural law principle."

The Society publishes a monograph on Self Defense and the Bible by the Rev. Anthony L. Winfield, an ordained Baptist Minister and former Marine.

Snyder, a former seminarian, insisted that the society "is international and interdenominational, since the principle of self-defense is universally accepted, but for Catholics (it) has particular credence because of Possenti."

Rather than "patron of self-defense," the society prefers "handgunners" because "he was proficient in the use of several kinds of firearms."

The Passionists, St. Gabriel's religious community, have no official recognition of the society or its cause, nor an official condemnation. Father Don Weber, first consultor of the Chicago Province of the Passionists, told the Register it was a "non-issue."

Father Sebastian McDonald, superior of a Passionist monastery near Detroit, explained that there are three problems with recognizing such a society.

First, he questioned the veracity of the handgun incident itself. He told the Register that Possenti biographer Father Poage, a peritus at the Second Vatican Council, is a holy priest but "an Irishman with a tremendous imagination, and a reputation for storytelling. Things he recounts as facts sometimes end up 60 percent true."

Many short biographies of Possenti's life don't mention the handgun incident. Snyder himself reports that on a recent pilgrimage to the saint's shrine in Isola, no literature was present that referred to the famous shot. The reason, Snyder claims, is a cover-up, especially as the entire year of 1860 in the saint's life seems to have been obliterated from official literature.

For a second reason, Father McDonald said the designation as patron of handgunners "would be misleading." Even if the lizard slaying did occur, it would be taking an incident in Possenti's life and politicizing it, and with a highly charged issue.

Snyder counters that the politicizing comes from the other side: "They are more concerned with being politically correct, than they are with being historically accurate…"

Father McDonald himself favors gun control but said that even some monks in his community have firearms for occasional rabbit-hunts on the monastery grounds.

The third reason, according to Father McDonald, is that naming a saint the "patron of handgunners" would be extrapolating a small incident in the saint's life and giving it too much importance. "His spiritual significance is far greater." He agreed to the analogy that it would be like Pope John Paul II, years hence, being remembered as a great skier.

Appendix E

American Handgunners To Seek Vatican Recognition

By Alberto Carosa

(Alberto Carosa is a distinguished Italian journalist. Versions of his article have appeared in the United States on the web site of the American Society for the Defense of Tradition, Family and Property, www.tfp.org, and in Brazil, in Portuguese, in the July, 2001 issue of Catolicismo. Reprinted here with permission of Mr. Carosa.)

ROME - From time to time the Catholic Church has to address the thorny problems caused by those liberal faithful who in one way or another challenge her principles and tenets. Much more rarely do we hear about initiatives coming from the other side of the spectrum, with the difference that these initiatives in general do not pose any threat to the Church doctrine, limiting the call to an extended application of existing principles. This is the approach of the St. Gabriel Possenti Society, Inc., which for the first time, came all the way to Rome, to plead for the official recognition by the Vatican of St. Gabriel Possenti as the Patron Saint of Handgunners.

The members of the US-based international and interdenominational St. Gabriel Possenti Society, Inc., uphold the right of law-abiding citizens to keep and bear arms to defend themselves against evil and tyranny. According to its founder-president, John Michael Snyder, there is nothing wrong in this, since he views the issue as an extension of the right to life. In his opinion, that's also why the Catholic Church, as a genuine and consistent defender of life, could speak out in favor of preserving the right to defend life, a struggle concomitant with the struggle to preserve the right to life.

A good first step in this direction would be precisely to proclaim St. Gabriel Possenti (1838-1862) Patron of Handgunners. To better press the issue, John Snyder presented special honor medallions to a select few recipients, who have demonstrated their commitment to the principle of defense of truth and justice against evil and tyranny, during an awards conference in the shadow of the Basilica of St Peter on February 27, 2001, the Feast Day of the Saint.

In 1860 St. Gabriel Possenti (in Italy better known as San Gabriele dell'Addolorata) rescued the villagers of Isola del Gran Sasso in the Abruzzo region from a gang of 20 armed renegades with a striking, one-shot, lizard-slaying demonstration of handgun marksmanship.

The Society also promotes the study and exposition of the historical, philosophical and theological bases for the doctrine of legitimate self-defense. To this end it distributes a monograph on Self Defense and the

Bible, by a Baptist author, the Rev. Anthony L. Winfield.

Thus far, the Vatican has not complied with the Society's request. While it may be true that some church officials get weak in the knees at the sound of, or even mention of the word of gunfire, the fact remains that the whole idea faced opposition since its very inception. As far back as the early 90s, the heads of the two Passionist US provinces (St. Gabriel was a member of the Passionist order) strongly protested the idea, on the sheer lack of historical evidence for the incident. More recently, in late 1997, Cardinal Roger Etchegaray, president of the Pontifical Council for Justice and Peace, waged a personal, public attack on the private possession of handguns or firearms of small caliber, claiming in some Council papers that limiting the purchase of handguns and small arms would certainly not infringe upon the rights of anyone and all firearms must remain under the strict control of the state.

Over the years John M. Snyder has been puzzled by the retreat of some churchmen on the Possenti-self-defense issue. Initially, some of them tried to say that the lizard incident never happened. When evidence was quoted, such as the account of the incident in Son of the Passion, by Rev. Godfrey Poage, C.P. (Milwaukee, Wisconsin, USA, Bruce Publishing Company, 1962), they said maybe it did not happen. The latest is that they are saying that if it did happen, it did not have much significance. When the Religious News Service in the United States brought this to the attention of Father

Poage, he said that he did the research for the book and he knows what happened and that his critics on this issue do not. The book carries the imprimatur of the Church and other official designations of approval.

As to Cardinal Etchegaray, in a subsequent letter John Snyder objected to his theses, saying that in the US alone, scores of millions of law-abiding citizens own firearms of various types and for a number of legitimate reasons. "There are more gun owners here than there are people who vote for the two majority party presidential candidates every four years," he notes. "Approximately 80 million law-abiding people own about 200 million handguns, rifles and shotguns and the available record indicates quite clearly that the ability of law-abiding citizens to possess firearms is a crime deterrent and a life saver." But Snyder was particularly critical of the idea of state-controlled firearms, since civilian disarmament has been one of the major factors leading to the horrible metastasis of government-sponsored genocide in the unfortunately bloody and murderous 20th century. As shown by Jay Simkin, Aaron Zelman and Alan M. Rice in Lethal Laws, published in 1994 in Milwaukee, Wisconsin, by Jews for the Preservation of Firearms Ownership, Inc., genocides perpetrated in at least seven cases, namely in Ottoman Turkey, Soviet Union, Nazi Germany with occupied Europe, China, Guatemala, Uganda and Cambodia, were all preceded by civilian disarmament. In each case, the civilian disarmament was preceded by the enactment of gun control legislation making possible the disarmament.

On the contrary Father Sebastian McDonald, superior of a Passionist monastery near Detroit, favors gun control and put forth three problems with recognizing the saint as Patron of Handgunners. First he questioned the veracity of the handgun incident itself, arguing that Father Poage, though a peritus (expert) at the Second Vatican Council and a holy priest, is an Irishman with a tremendous imagination and a reputation for story telling. Secondly, the designation as patron would be misleading and third would be extrapolating a small incident in the saint's life and giving it too much importance.

Snyder's reaction to this is that the "good father" and "others like him" are "more concerned with being politically correct than they are with being historically accurate."

Snyder maintains that the St. Gabriel Possenti Society, Inc. is not a lobby as the term is understood in American law. It does not officially support or oppose specific pieces of legislation or candidates for public office. Nonetheless, the clout and influence of over 80 million gun owners in the US is undeniable. Not many years ago a madman in Killeen, Texas, murdered a number of innocent customers in a cafeteria, including the parents of Suzanna Gratia Hupp. She owned a handgun, which she had to leave in her automobile because at that time Texas did not permit the carrying of concealed handguns, and contended that she could have saved her parents and others, had she had the handgun with her. At around that same time as the cafeteria killing, Governor Ann Richards vetoed a bill to mandate the issuance of permits to carry concealed firearms to law-abiding applicants. Her political opponent campaigned against her on that issue and won the election. The new governor signed into law a similar bill: his name was George W. Bush.

To obtain additional copies of GUN SAINT by John Michael Snyder, including information on bulk orders, please contact the publisher at 703-418-0849.